LIFE LAID BARE

THE SURVIVORS IN RWANDA SPEAK

JEAN HATZFELD

translated from the French by Linda Coverdale

OTHER PRESS · NEW YORK

Production Editor: Robert D. Hack

Text design by Jeremy Diamond
This book was set in 10.2 Janson Text by Alpha Graphics of Pittsfield, New Hampshire.

10 9 8 7 6 5 4 3 2 1

Library of Congress Cataloging-in-Publication Data

Hatzfeld, Jean.
   [Dans le nu de la vie. English]
   Life laid bare : the survivors in Rwanda speak / Jean Hatzfeld ;
translated from the French by Linda Coverdale.
       p. cm.
   Includes bibliographical references.
   ISBN-13: 978-1-59051-273-9 (pbk. : alk. paper)   1. Genocide–Rwanda.
2. Tutsi (African people)–Crimes against—Rwanda.   3. Tutsi (African
people)–Interviews.   4. Rwanda–History–Civil War, 1994–Atrocities.
I. Title.
   DT450.435.H3813 2007
   967.57104'31–dc22

                                    2007013924

ADVANCE PRAISE FOR
LIFE LAID BARE

"Jean Hatzfeld's *Machete Season*, wherein the perpetrators of the Rwandan genocide spoke about their crimes, was an astonishing feat of reportage and oral history. *Life Laid Bare*, which allows the victims to speak, is an even greater achievement—a book so elegantly wrought, so unexpected and revelatory, that it's absolutely essential reading in understanding what happened in Rwanda, how the survivors of genocide find a way to begin again while never forgetting to bear witness. As Marie-Louise Kagoyire, one of the narrators says, '[S]howing our hearts to a stranger, talking about how we feel, laying bare our feelings as survivors, that shocks us beyond measure.'"

—DAVE EGGERS, author of *What Is the What*

"Of all the books I have read about the genocide in Rwanda—and I have read many good ones—*Life Laid Bare* is unique. Hatzfeld has a talent for letting the voices of the victims speak directly to us with no apparent mediation. These voices laid bare tell their stories in such a matter-of-fact manner that all explanatory discourses become redundant. One comes out of this harrowing and perversely fascinating book completely devastated, wondering whether this thing we call 'human' in us does really exist."

—EMMANUEL DONGALA, author of *Johnny Mad Dog*

"Arresting firsthand accounts of the 1994 Rwandan genocide from 14 men, women, and children who survived the weeks of slaughter. As he did in *Machete Season: The Killers in Rwanda Speak* (2005), journalist Hatzfeld provides informative introductions to each chapter but allows his subjects to speak for themselves. The collection's devastating power comes from the no-holds-barred narratives, with additional kudos to translator Coverdale for rendering their words in spare, haunting English. . . . The details may change, but for the Rwandan survivors, the memories themselves will never disappear. Hatzfeld is to be commended for helping to preserve crucial eyewitness testimony and for sharing it with what one hopes will be a very large audience."

—*Kirkus Reviews*

CONTENTS

MAP OF RWANDA

MAP OF THE DISTRICT OF NYAMATA

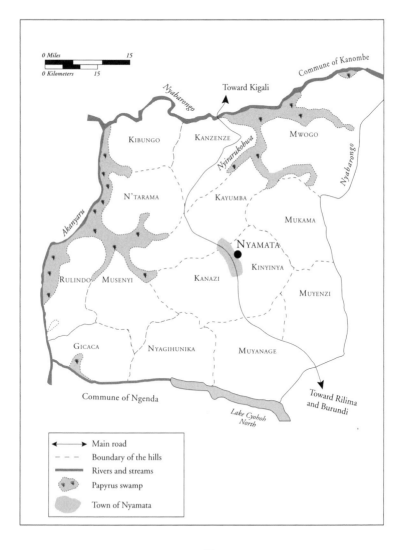

0 Miles 15
0 Kilometers 15

Commune of Kanombe

Nyabarongo

Toward Kigali

KIBUNGO   KANZENZE   MWOGO

Nyirarukobwa

Nyabarongo

N'TARAMA   KAYUMBA

Akanyaru

MUKAMA

NYAMATA

KINYINYA

RULINDO   MUSENYI   KANAZI

MUYENZI

GICACA   NYAGIHUNIKA   MUYANAGE

Commune of Ngenda

Toward Rilima
and Burundi

*Lake Cyohoh
North*

Main road
Boundary of the hills
Rivers and streams
Papyrus swamp
Town of Nyamata

CHRONOLOGY OF EVENTS
IN RWANDA AND
THE DISTRICT OF NYAMATA

1921 Under a League of Nations mandate, Rwanda and Burundi, formerly part of German East Africa and occupied by Belgian troops during World War I, fall under Belgian rule.

1931 Identity cards specifying the ethnic group of the bearer are introduced, a policy continued until 1994.

1946 Rwanda becomes a UN trust territory and is administered as a Belgian colony and part of Congo.

1959 The last great Tutsi king, Mutara Rudahigwa, dies. The Hutu peasant massacres and revolts that follow cause the exodus of hundreds of thousands of Tutsis.

1960 The Belgian Congo becomes independent, and Rwanda becomes a republic.

1961 The Hutu political parties achieve victory in Rwanda's first legislative elections.

1962 The independence of Rwanda is proclaimed.

1963 In Nyamata, the Rwandan army carries out the first widespread massacres of Tutsis.

1973 Major Juvénal Habyarimana carries out a military coup d'état. Large numbers of Hutus fleeing poverty and drought flood into Nyamata, where renewed and repeated massacres occur.

1978 Juvénal Habyarimana is elected president.

1990 The Tutsi-led Rwandan Patriotic Front, which has been assembled from Tutsi militias operating out of Tanzania, Uganda, Burundi, and Zaire, gains its first military victories in Rwanda. Hutu extremist militias, called *interahamwe*, are organized by the Habyarimana clan.

1993 A peace agreement is signed in Arusha, Tanzania, between Habyarimana's regime and the RPF.

1994 APRIL 6, 8 P.M. Habyarimana is assassinated when his plane is brought down by a mysterious missile on its approach to Kigali Airport.

APRIL 7, EARLY MORNING. Assassinations begin of political figures who did not fully support Habyarimana's dictatorship; the victims include Prime Minister Agathe Uwilingiyimana, a Hutu.

RPF forces immediately begin their drive toward the capital, Kigali, where Hutu *interahamwe* militias have started slaughtering Tutsis and moderate Hutus. The genocide begins; it will continue for about a hundred days. In Nyamata, small-scale violence breaks out, definitively separating the two ethnic communities on the hills.

APRIL 9. In Nyamata *interahamwe* troops launch the first raids to loot and burn houses abandoned by Tutsis and to murder rebellious Hutus; local farmers help them, but without receiving specific orders.

APRIL 11. After waiting four days for directions from the government, Hutu soldiers from the base at Gako begin systematic killings in the streets of Nyamata. On the hills, the local authorities and *interahamwe* assemble the farmers, and their planned attacks on Tutsis begin.

APRIL 14–15. In Nyamata approximately five thousand Tutsi refugees are massacred by machete, first in the church, then in the Sainte-Marthe Maternity Hospital.

APRIL 15. Some five thousand refugees are massacred in the church in N'tarama, nineteen miles from Nyamata.

APRIL 16. Organized hunts for Tutsis begin in the marshes of Nyamwiza and on the hill of Kayumba—wherever Tutsis have sought refuge.

MAY 12. Tens of thousands of Hutu families start fleeing toward Congo on the Gitarama road. The genocide in Nyamata is over.

MAY 14. The RPF reaches Nyamata and begins to look for survivors in the marshes.

JULY 4. Kigali falls to the RPF, which installs a new government with a Hutu president and General Paul Kagame as minister of defense. The RPF will eventually be reorganized into the regular Rwandan army.

JULY 15. Half a million Hutu refugees begin to cross the border into Congo; eventually some 1.7 million Hutus fill the refugee camps of eastern Congo.

OCTOBER 3. The United Nations Security Council endorses a report describing the massacres committed in Rwanda as genocide.

1996 NOVEMBER. Rebel forces opposing President Mobutu Sese Seko's regime invade eastern Congo, supported by Rwandan forces. Tens of thousands of Hutu refugees are killed, and some two million refugees eventually return to Rwanda. Most *interahamwe* either were killed during this Rwandan offensive or joined the return and gave themselves up to the Rwandan government, but some still live in Congo, in bands of looters or mercenaries, mostly in the Kivu region on the border.

1997 MAY 17. Troops of the Rwandan army sweep through Congo, driving out Mobutu and bringing Laurent-Désiré Kabila to power in Kinshasa.

1998 APRIL 24. In Nyamata six condemned prisoners are publicly executed on the hill of Kayumba—to this day, the sole official executions there.

2002 JANUARY 1. The Third Republic is proclaimed in Rwanda, consolidating the regime of President Paul Kagame, who has been the strong man of the RPF from the start.

AUGUST. *Gaçaça*[1] courts begin operating in Nyamata.

2003 JANUARY 1. A presidential decree is issued concerning those convicted of crimes of genocide. It authorizes the release of elderly and sick prisoners and allows probation—in conjunction with three days of communal labor per week—for convicts in the second and third categories (lower-echelon killers and their accomplices) whose confessions have been accepted and who have already served at least half their prison sentences.

LIFE LAID BARE

INTRODUCTION

In 1994, between eleven in the morning on Monday, April 11 and two in the afternoon on Saturday, May 14, about fifty thousand Tutsis, out of a population of around fifty-nine thousand, were massacred by machete, murdered every day of the week, from nine-thirty in the morning until four in the afternoon, by Hutu neighbors and militiamen, on the hills of the district of Nyamata, in Rwanda. That is the point of departure of this book.

A few days earlier, on the evening of April 6, 1994, a plane carrying Juvénal Habyarimana, the president of the Republic of Rwanda, had exploded on its approach to the airport in Kigali. This attack was the signal to begin killing the Tutsi population, a slaughter that had been planned for months and started at dawn in the streets of the capital, spreading quickly throughout the land.

Four days later, amid the hills and marshes of the Bugesera region, the killing began on the main street of the little town of Nyamata. Throngs of Tutsis immediately sought refuge in churches or fled into banana groves, swamps, and forests of eucalyptus. On April 14, 15, and 16, five thousand people in the church at Nyamata and as many again in the church at N'tarama, a hamlet twelve miles away, were murdered by militiamen, soldiers, and the vast majority of their Hutu neighbors. Those two massacres unleashed the genocide in this arid region of red clay laterite, where the killing went on until mid-May. For a month, singing as they went, disciplined gangs of dedicated killers armed with machetes, spears, and clubs tracked down and surrounded those fleeing through the papyrus swamps of Nyamwiza and the eucalyptus forests of Kayumba. These diligent hunters killed five out of six Tutsis, the same percentage that perished throughout the rest of the Rwandan countryside, and a much higher proportion than died in the cities.

For several years the survivors of the Nyamata hills, like their fellows throughout Rwanda, have lived in a muteness as enigmatic as the silence of those who survived the Nazi concentration camps. Today, some Tutsis explain that "life has broken down," whereas for others, it has "stopped," and still others say that it "absolutely must go on." They all admit, however, that among themselves they talk of nothing but the genocide. That was what convinced me to return to Rwanda and speak with them, to drink Primus beer in Marie-Louise's shop or banana beer at the bar in Kibungo, to keep visiting the adobe houses and *cabaret*[2] terraces, to chat in the shade of the acacias, hesitantly at first, then with increasing confidence and familiarity, meeting Cassius, Francine, Angélique, Berthe, and the others, to persuade them to tell their stories. Some of them seemed doubtful about why they should talk to a foreigner, or why a foreigner might listen to them, but no one turned me down.

To explain such a long silence on their part, they also said, for example, that they had found themselves "shouldered aside," as if they were now "in the way." Or that they "distrusted people," that they were too discouraged, isolated, "undone." That they felt "uneasy" or sometimes "at fault" as well, for having taken the place of someone they'd known, or for rejoining the daily world of the living.

Herders, farmwomen, teachers, tradeswomen, a social worker, a mason's helper: day after day, in Nyamata or up in the surrounding hills, they told their stories, at the mercy of their misgivings or their difficulties in evoking certain memories, and led on by new questions inspired by their testimony. Most of them, skeptical or indifferent before the lessons of history, are tempted in spite of everything to share with others how incomprehensible, distressing, and lonely their lives have become.

A genocide is not a particularly cruel and murderous war. It is a project of extermination. In the aftermath of a war, civilian survivors feel a strong need to bear witness; in the wake of a genocide, on the other hand, the survivors yearn strangely for silence. Their withdrawal is disturbing.

The history of the Rwandan genocide will take a long time to write. The object of this book is not, however, to join the stack of documents, inquiries, and novels (some of them excellent) already published. It is solely to bring readers the astonishing stories of these survivors.

A genocide is—to summarize one survivor's own definition—an inhuman undertaking conceived by human beings, a project too methodical and insane to be fathomed. And yet, the accounts of headlong flight through the marshes by Claudine, Odette, Jean-Baptiste, Christine, and their neighbors; the descriptions—often bluntly and magnificently expressed—of their crude encampments, their increasing degradation, humiliation, and finally their marginalization by Rwandan society; their apprehensions regarding the way other people see them, their obsessions, complicities, their explorations and interrogations of their own memories, and their reflections as survivors, but also as Africans and villagers, allow us to draw as close as we can get to the Rwandan genocide.

EARLY MORNING IN NYAMATA

Gray cranes, with their trumpeting calls, are the first to announce that nighttime is over in the neighborhood of Gatare. Like big green parrots, turacos with impressive white crests soon add their squawking, and sunrise will not be long now. In the morning mist appear woolly necked storks on the wing and patrolling pelicans, gliding hesitantly above the ponds. Some goats then demand to leave their pens of branches nestled against the houses, and the new day gets underway when the cattle disappear one by one, or in small herds, into the bush of Kayumba, prodded by the long staves of bare-chested boys in jackets too big for them.

Lined with mud dwellings, the last lanes and alleys on the upper slopes of the neighborhood straggle along toward some wasteland with a soccer field at one end, which also marks the end of the main street of Nyamata. Muddy in the rainy season and heat-warped in dry weather, this field equipped with cast-iron goal posts never discourages the players of all ages who come and go throughout the day. In the lower section of Gatare there is a scattering of more solidly constructed houses, the homes of many teachers, shopkeepers, and magistrates.

There Édith Uwanyiligira presides over a brick guesthouse in the shade of a small grove of mango and papaya trees. The large courtyard in the rear is invaded from dawn to dusk by a whole swarm of local kids who line up single file, between the kitchen hut and the small shanty for the household help, to fill their jerry cans with water at the only working faucet in the neighborhood. The children gather in this courtyard at mealtimes, attracted by a big-bellied cooking pot that simmers all day, fed by the wheelbarrows of vegetables fetched from the market by the proprietress.

From the veranda you can hear, on the right, the songs of the large-beaked tomakos and the dovelike, linden green couroucous perched in the trees. Across the way are dilapidated clay and straw houses, small gardens planted with beans, and some deep ditches where straw and dried mud are formed into bricks. Chickens wander about; washing hangs from branches and hedges.

A road, quickly thronged with pedestrians, bicyclists, and lucky moped riders, runs past the yellow town hall surrounded by its high flowering hedge. In the courtyard, local officials in white shirts talk with villagers looking to get papers stamped. In the parking lot sit the mayor's all-terrain van, the tractor that collects the town trash, and a crowd of bicycles and mopeds leaning in clusters against the avocado trees.

The town hall is where Innocent Rwililiza works, and a few hundred yards away is the austerely furnished office of Sylvie Umubyeyi.

Sylvie Umubyeyi is a social worker, and thus the first person whom I come to know in Nyamata. After learning in Kigali that some child survivors are living in little "families" in the bush around the marshes in the Nyamata area, I go to see Sylvie to ask her if I might manage to meet these children. Skeptical, or suspicious, she does not want to help a foreigner make such direct contact with them. On my way back to Kigali, however, I run into Sylvie at the entrance to the Memorial,[3] where we chat for a moment, and this chance encounter seems to change her mind. Without any explanation, she promptly suggests that I come along in her van while she visits some banana groves. She introduces me to Jeannette Ayinkamiye, a teenage farmer who takes care of some abandoned children, with whom we spend a morning talking. Sylvie takes me up into the hills several times, and she also agrees to talk about herself, cautiously at first, then willingly and regularly. She is enthralling, and so I decide to focus on the hills of Nyamata.

During my next visit, Sylvie asks Innocent Rwililiza to lend a hand; he, too, turns out to be an attentive and understanding companion. Both of them become guides and friends, without whom all these expeditions into the hills and meetings with survivors would not be possible.

On many occasions they both prove to be invaluable and skilled interpreters as well. I must point out that these accounts are given in three languages: Kinyarwanda, the native tongue of the farmers; Rwandan French, the second language of the other witnesses and the translators; and standard

French. The Rwandan French—which appropriates French vocabulary magnificently—faithfully captures certain thoughts and descriptions, and has been carefully respected, although it does lead to a few surprising and surely excusable linguistic formulations.

Leaving the town, the road turns left, entering the grounds of what was once the parish church. This church was the only architecturally modern building in the town, but today its gaping walls and pock-marked roof show the damage left by exploding grenades. The Vatican Curia made plans several times to restore the church and reopen it for religious services, but the inhabitants of Nyamata decided to keep it in its present state and build one of the region's two memorials there. For this was the site of the first massacre of a crowd of five thousand people, which turned loose the hunters of men throughout the Bugesera.

Within the church park, goats browse on bushes, watched over by a twelve-year-old boy. He sits in the shade of a tree, a switch in his hand, a soccer ball at his feet, chatting with the caretaker of the Memorial. His name is Cassius Niyonsaba. He can be found every day of the week hanging out at the church, which is halfway between his school and the home of his Aunt Thérèse. He comes here occasionally to kick the ball around with a pal. At times he is surrounded by his goats, as today, while at others he sits alone on the low wall behind the church, staring at a burial vault. Slicing through his frizzy hair, a deep scar runs the entire length of his skull.

CASSIUS NIYONSABA,

12 Years Old, Schoolboy
N'tarama Hill

Papa was a primary school teacher, Mama a farmer. In my father's family, it's only me who's still alive. In my mother's family, it's just only me as well, who's still alive. I no longer remember how many big and little brothers and sisters I had, because my memory is too taken up by so many deaths, it's not handy with numbers anymore. That slows me down in school, too.

But I can relive in full transparency the massacres in the church and the ferociousness of the *interahamwe*.[4] That's what the Hutu killers are called. We'd grown used to passing them on the road. They would shout noisy threats at us. We heard them, we did say to ourselves that things weren't going well, but still, we couldn't actually believe it. Later on, after the plane crash, the neighboring Hutus on my hill came every day to kill people where they lived, without even waiting for an ordinary argument or quarrel. So people understood that this was no joke and they slipped off to the forest or the church.

Me, I went down to my big sister's place in Nyamata—reason why I didn't die in N'tarama.

The day the killing began in Nyamata, in the big market street, we ran to the parish church. A great crowd had already gathered, because it's part of Rwandan custom to take refuge in God's houses when the massacres begin. Time let us have two days of quiet, then the soldiers and local police came to patrol around the church, yelling that we really were all going to be killed. We hardly dared talk, or breathe—I can remember that. It was not yet noon when the *interahamwe* arrived singing: they threw grenades, they tore down the railings, then they rushed into the church and started slicing people up with machetes and spears. They wore manioc leaves in their hair, they shouted full force, laughed with all their heart. They struck with swinging arms. They cut anyone, without choosing.

People not streaming with their own blood were streaming with the blood of others, oh it was something. So, then, they started dying without resisting anymore. There was a huge uproar and a huge silence at the same time. In the thick of the afternoon, the *interahamwe* burned little children in front of the door. I saw them with my own eyes turning and twisting from burning truly completely alive. There was a strong smell of meat, and of gasoline.

I'd lost all track of my big sister, I was stunned beyond bewilderment. Toward the end of the afternoon, I was hit with a hammer: I fell, but I managed to snake my way over to hide with some boys behind a metal gate. When the *interahamwe* had finished work for the day, some young guys from home, still strong enough to escape into the bush, carried me off on their backs.

The *interahamwe* finished up the killing in the church in two days, and right away they came tracking after us into the forest with clubs and machetes. Led by their dogs they came searching for fugitives beneath the branches. That's where I was caught. I heard a shout, I saw a machete, I was bashed on the head, and I fell into a hollow.

At first I ought to have been dead, then I insisted on living, but I don't remember how. A lady passing by, first-named Mathilde, found me and took me away to a hiding place beneath some *umunzenze*. *Umunzenze* are giant trees. Each evening, in the darkness, she would bring me water and some food. My head was rotting—I could feel worms that seemed to be gnawing near my brain. I thought an evil spell was preying on me. But the lady put leaves, some African medicine, over the wound. This good-hearted lady was from Nyamata. I didn't know her by her full name, because I was from N'tarama, as I already told you. She was simply Tutsi, the wife of a Hutu administrator. I found out afterward that when her husband learned she had taken care of a Tutsi child, he took her to the edge of the pond at Rwaki-Birizi, a good half-mile away, and he killed her with a knife, in one thrust. Later, he joined the procession of those fleeing to Congo, and no one has ever seen him since.

I no longer remember properly the end of the genocide, because of my cut on the head. My strength was gone, almost all my thoughts were gone, and even the roof of the family house was gone. I was very low with malaria, with only a pair of shorts to wear. I had no one left to go with, since everyone close had been killed, at the church or in the marshes. So, I went back to live in Nyamata, back to the house of my Aunt Thérèse, who just farms.

Now I live among her children, and other children on their own like me. When we children talk, someone may mention the genocide, so then each one starts to tell what he saw. That can take a long time. Now and then someone wants to change a detail, but usually we repeat the same memories to one another. Talking together clears away pain and sadness.

I went back to school, in the fourth grade. There are Hutu children on the benches, and I have no problems with them. Sometimes I play with the soccer ball a little, but it's mostly the boys from Burundi who bring the ball and put on slippers to kick it around. What I like is talking with a pal, and going for walks. I run into a little fear only if I go alone to fetch firewood far from the houses, on account of the families that returned from Congo. When my turn comes to watch Auntie's goats, I take them into the bush with the cowherds and their animals.

But what I love best, it's to spend snatches of time in the church courtyard. In the place where I escaped the massacres. Every day I go there, it's on the way to school. Saturdays and holidays, I go as well. Sometimes I drive my aunt's goats, or I bring along a friend with a ball, or I sit by myself. I look at the holes in the wall every day. I go over to the niches to look at the skulls, the bones that used to be all those people killed around me.

At the beginning, I felt inclined to cry, seeing those skulls without names or eyes, looking at me. But little by little you get used to it. I sit there for a long time, and my thoughts go off with all of them. I try not to imagine personal faces when I look at the skulls, because if I happen to think about someone I know, then fear grabs me. I simply travel in memory among all those dead who were scattered around and didn't get buried. The sight and smell of the bones hurt me and at the same time, they comfort my mind. They stir up my thoughts, anyway.

In school, there's no time to talk seriously about all this. I also hear a lot of people who urge me to let go of my memories, as harmful things. Reason why I come back to the church. I like this peacefulness. After school, I like to swap long reflections with the caretaker of the Memorial. His name is Épimaque Rwema. He tells me how before the genocide Nyamata was a good town with lots of businesses, a really strong soccer team, cars in the street, and how life seemed peaceful and only hard during droughts. How people lowered themselves into the mud during the genocide, and why neighbors won't speak to one another with words open to pity anymore. He explains to me why some people are crushed in spite of their deliverance. He also tells me about the foreigners of good faith who now come to visit the bones at the Memorial— he even talks about the ones who forget to leave little gifts.

I hear that there were killings everywhere in the Bugesera and the country, but the ones in Nyamata were a little more shocking because the criminals hacked up women and children even at the foot of the cross. That's why the authorities gave us permission to build a memorial.

In the church, I did in fact recognize one neighbor who was clubbing away, he was from N'tarama. He was pounding as if he couldn't stop himself anymore. He was panting beyond breathless. He had no shirt, sweat was dripping from all over him, even though he was working his club well in the shade of the roof. Often, near the market, I encounter his family: they came back to his plot of land, and that bothers me. I know he is locked up in the prison at Rilima. I think he cannot live anymore, because someone who has struck too much with his club, he no longer thinks of anything but those he killed, and how he killed them, and he will nevermore lose the appetite for killing. At the church, I saw how savagery can replace kindness in the heart of a man, faster than a driving rain. Now that painful anxiety upsets me.

I think that never will the Whites, or even the Blacks of neighboring countries, come to believe the whole of what happened in our land. They will accept pieces of truth but ignore the rest. Even among ourselves, we are startled to hear of the killings we weren't there for, as they're told to us by friends, because the real truth about the killings of Tutsis—it's too much for one and all of us alike. Reason why, when I think about those who cut Papa and Mama, and all my kin, I'd like them to be shot, so as to draw my thoughts away from my family's miserable end.

I personally think the *interahamwe* can't offer a single good explanation for why they hate Tutsis. They only know how to repeat the same old threats or accusations. Supposedly, they're afraid of something hidden in the Tutsi character, a danger in disguise. The truth, it's that they're too much on the lookout for Tutsi riches, they're afraid of running short of farming plots one day, and they fear they'll all become our beggars. Even when Tutsis are poorer than they are, Hutus want to dig in their houses to take their bits of nothing-at-all. Hutus have rotted their own hearts with greed and propaganda.

When I grow up, I won't go to Mass anymore. I'll never go inside another church. I would like to be a teacher, because in school I can take comfort from other people, and because Papa was a teacher.

THE BIG AND LITTLE MARKETS

A hundred yards from the church appears the main street of Nyamata, lined with majestic *umuniyinya*, known as "palaver trees." A wooden sign for an AIDS-awareness campaign, the only advertising in town, marks the entrance to the marketplace, where soccer players orbit around balls made of banana leaves, pausing only during the high heat of siesta time.

Nyamata lives to the rhythm of two markets, large and small. The big one is held on Wednesdays and Saturdays, when, as day dawns, market women arrange their merchandise on cloths spread over the ground. As in all of Africa, the market is laid out by professions. In one corner gather the fishermen's wives, near their smoked or dried fish strung on vines and protected from flies by a film of dust. Elsewhere, farm women offer their stems of bananas, mounds of yams, and bags of red beans. Farther along are heaps of shoes, old or new, single or in pairs. Sumptuous displays of cloth from Taiwan or Congo for *pagnes*—wraparound skirts—sit next to stacks of T-shirts and underwear.

From early morning on, the crowd leaves little room to maneuver for the porters' slender wooden wheelbarrows or the women bearing wicker trays, who replenish the stocks of merchandise. Music is sold a little off to one side, in the street. The shop consists of a cassette player sitting on a stool, for sampling, and three tables covered with tapes of hymns, folk melodies from the African Great Lakes Region, the melancholy songs of the popular Rwandan singer Annonciata Kamaliza, plus more lively hits from Congo and South Africa. Céline Dion and Julio Iglesias bring music from the world at large.

This market is rather cheerful and modest (not to say meager), without any jewelry, musical instruments, second-hand dealers, sellers of paintings or sculptures, without much haggling or chatter, or too many disruptive scenes, either.

As for the little market, it is essentially alimentary and is held every day on some bumpy wasteland behind the square. Heaps of manioc surround the milling shed. Goats are for sale near the slaughterhouse, the front of which serves as a butcher's stall. Not far away are the veterinary pharmacy and clinic, and the *cabaret* frequented by the local vets. Charcoal is sold near stacks of firewood. One may also find peat, manure, the men who resole flipflops, jerry cans of banana beer, jugs of milk curds, piles of trussed chickens, pyramids of salt and sugar, and the ubiquitous sacks of beans.

The marketplace is surrounded by stores painted green, blue, and orange, colors faded by the heat and dust. Half the shops are closed and have been falling apart since the war. The others house hairdressers' salons and dim *cabarets* where men nurse their banana beers. In Nyamata, there are no more newspaper stands, and the only bookstore left is the religious one, where people go to get photocopies. Beneath the shop awnings, near the displays of fabric and the photography studios, seamstresses bend over their black and gold sewing machines, splendid Singers or Butterflys. They mend a torn pair of trousers, cut shirts to measure, hem cloth for pagnes, all in the time it takes their customers to visit the church, the health center, or the town hall.

Twice a week, Jeannette Ayinkamiye comes down from the hill of Kanazi to sew in the marketplace, among twenty or so machines that click along in a diligent silence interrupted now and then by laughter or consultations. On those days, Jeannette wears her long Sunday dress with puffy sleeves, but no jewelry, braids, or curls, which are forbidden by her Pentecostal pastor.

The rest of the week, except for Sunday, she farms a family plot. She abandoned her studies after the genocide. She lives in a spotless brick house with two younger sisters and two orphans in her care, whom she feeds, clothes, and sends to school. She had never spoken with a foreigner before, but at our first meeting, she agrees without hesitation to tell her story. Whenever she speaks, painfully and repeatedly, about the death of her mother, she seems courageously determined to carry on.

JEANNETTE AYINKAMIYE,
17 Years Old, Farmer and Seamstress
Kinyinya Hill (Maranyundo)

I was born among seven brothers and two sisters. Papa was cut down on the first day, but we never learned where. My brothers were killed not long afterward. Mama and my little sisters and I managed to flee into the marshes. We lasted a month beneath the papyrus fronds, almost without seeing or hearing anything of the world anymore.

During the day, we lay stretched in the mud with the snakes and mosquitoes to hide from the attacks of the *interahamwe*. At night we wandered among abandoned houses to find something to eat in the farming plots. Because we lived only on what we found, there were many bouts of diarrhea, but luckily the usual diseases, malaria or rain fevers, seemed willing to spare us for once. We knew nothing anymore about life, except that the Tutsis had been massacred throughout the country and that we ourselves would soon die.

We usually hid in small groups. One day the *interahamwe* unearthed Mama beneath the papyrus. She stood up; she offered them money to kill her with a single machete blow.

They stripped her to take the money knotted up in her pagne. They chopped both her arms off first, then her legs. Mama was murmuring, "Saint Cécile, Saint Cécile," but she didn't beg for mercy.

Thinking about this makes me sad. But it grieves me whether I remember it in my thoughts or out loud, that's why I don't mind telling you about it.

My two little sisters saw everything because they were lying beside her. They were struck too: Vanessa on the ankles, Marie-Claire on the head. The killers did not cut them completely to pieces. Perhaps because they were in a hurry, perhaps they did it on purpose, as with Mama. I myself only heard the noises and screams, because I was concealed in a hole nearby. When the *interahamwe* had gone, I came out and gave Mama a taste of water.

The first evening she could still speak. She told me, "Jeannette, I am leaving without hope, because I think you will follow me." She was suffering greatly from the cuttings, but she kept saying that we would all die, and that grieved her even more. I did not dare spend the night with her. I first had to take care of my little sisters, who were badly hurt but not dying. The next day, it was not possible to stay with her either, since we had to hide. That was the rule in the marshes: anyone who was seriously cut had to be abandoned, for safety's sake.

Mama lay in agony for three days before dying at last. On the second day, she could only whisper, "Goodbye, children," and ask for water, but she still could not let go. I wasn't able to stay by her for long because of the *interahamwe* attacks. I saw that it was all over for her. I also understood that for some people, bereft of everything, for whom suffering had become the last companion, death must really have been too long a task, and so useless. On the third day, she could no longer swallow, only moan a few little words, and look around. She never closed her eyes again. Her name was Agnès Nyira-buguzi. In Kinyarwanda, Nyirabuguzi means "Mother of many."

Now I often dream about her in a vivid scene deep in the marsh. I gaze at Mama's face, I listen to her words, I give her something to drink but the water won't go down her throat anymore and flows away from her lips. Then the hunters return to the attack: I stand up, I start to run, but when I get back to the marsh and ask people about Mama, no one knows her as my mama anymore. That's when I wake up.

On the last day of the genocide, when the liberators called to us from the edges of the marsh, some of us refused to budge from under the papyrus, thinking this must be a new trick by the *interahamwe*. Afterward, in the evening, we were assembled on the soccer field in Nyamata. Those who were strong enough went off to rummage through houses for decent clothing. Even though we could at last eat proper food with salt, we showed no rejoicing, for our thoughts were with those whom we had left behind out there. We felt as we had in the marshes, save that no one was chasing us anymore. The danger of death was gone, but had left us still beaten down by life.

My little sisters' wounds were infected, so we sought shel-ter. The girls spent three weeks with the lady doctors before we could set out for home, where we found our house in ruins.

In the bush, we met up with Chantal Mukashema and her young cousin Jean-de-Dieu Murengerani, called Walli. We gathered in an uncle's house that had been looted, left with no roof, no bed, not even a scrap of cloth. There, our lives began again.

Now, we grow crops on our land. We prepare meals, laughing when we can, to bring the children closer to cheerfulness. But we don't celebrate birthdays anymore, because that pains us so, and it costs too much money. We've never quarreled with one another, not even once by accident, because we can't see why or how we would. Sometimes we sing ourselves songs from school. The two little girls have gone back to class. As for Jean-de-Dieu, he's too thoughtful ever since he was hacked on the head with a machete. He likes just to sit, chin in hand, without counting the hours. One day Chantal went off to marry someone named François, but we visit one another. Me, I don't see myself marrying, because of my little sisters and other obstacles. I come up against too many hesitations all around me. Actually, I don't feel that comfortable with life. I cannot think beyond the present anymore.

Last year, Uncle's house was falling apart. We were moved to Kanazi, into this sturdy home of bricks and sheet metal,[5] with a table, some chairs, and platform beds with drawers. Here, I am less troubled by my gloomy thoughts. On Mondays, Tuesdays, Thursdays, I farm our plots or those of neighbors who give me food or a few small coins. Wednesdays and Saturdays I go to the market in Nyamata, to sew on a Butterfly machine. A girl, Angélique, made a place for me next to her. I sew little repairs for passing customers, I get by with that. I regret not being able to learn the sewing profession properly, so as to give up farming.

The children have swept much misery from their minds, but they still have scars and headaches and thought-aches. When they suffer overmuch, we take the time to look back on those unhappy days. The two girls have the most to say, because with Mama, they saw it all. They often talk about the same scene and forget the rest.

Our memory changes with time. We forget details, we confuse dates, we mix up attacks, we make mistakes with names, we even disagree about how this or that man or woman and other acquaintances died. But we remember all the fearsome moments we personally lived through as if they had happened just last year. Time passes, but we keep our lists of specific memories and speak of them together when things are going badly; these memories become ever more truthful, yet we hardly know how to arrange them in the right order anymore.

When I find myself alone out in the field, I'm inclined at times to think back on such things too sadly. Then I set down my hoe and go to chat with some neighbors. We sing, we share some juice, and that does me good. On Sundays I attend church, I sing and pray. I think that Satan chose the Hutus to commit all those horrors simply because they were stronger and more numerous, and thus could spread more evil in just a few short months. When I hear on the radio about these African wars, I worry terribly. I think Satan takes advantage of God's all too long absences from Africa to multiply these great slaughters. I only hope that the souls of all Africans who have endured those calamities are welcomed with the proper grace.

The story of the Hutus and Tutsis is like that of Cain and Abel, brothers who cannot abide each other anymore because of mere nothings. But I do not believe the Tutsis resemble the Jews, even though both peoples were caught up in genocides. The Tutsis have never been a people chosen to hear the voice of God, the way the Hebrews were in pagan days. The Tutsis are not a people punished for the death of Jesus Christ. They are simply a people come to misfortune on the hills because of their noble bearing.

Out in the marsh, Vanessa looked a long moment into the eyes of Mama's murderers. Two years later, she recognized the face of one of those criminals, coming calmly back from Congo with his bundle of belongings. It was a lanky boy from Kayumba, he even had years of good schooling, our pastor's eldest son. He is doing time now in the penitentiary at Rilima, near Lake Kidogo.

Those inmates are an anguishing problem. If we imprison all the hatred of the slaughterers, it can never dry up in the open air. But if we let it seep back into the banana groves, the killings will begin again. I have seen women hurl themselves into the river, clutching children in their arms, to spare them the blood. Women above all, because women and children had to face more torment than the men. I know that if God does not Himself catch up with their killers to rebuke them, they will always want to do it again. I put my trust in Him because I cannot bear that anguish.

I know, myself, that when you have seen your mama cut so wickedly, and suffer so slowly, you become forever less trusting toward people, and not just the *interahamwe*. I mean that someone who has seen atrocious suffering for so long can never again live among others as before, because this person will remain on guard, suspicious of people, even if they have done nothing. I am saying that Mama's death brought me the most sorrow, but that her overlong agony did me the most damage, and that now this can never be fixed.

I also know, for the future, that a man can become unspeakably vicious in no time. I do not believe in the end of genocides. I do not believe those who say that we have seen the worst of atrocities for the last time. When a genocide has been committed, another one can come, no matter when, no matter where, in Rwanda or anyplace, if the root cause is still there and still unknown.

THE BUGESERA ROAD

To go to the Bugesera from Kigali, you take a wide avenue, always deafening and congested, that zigzags along to the highway to Tanzania. As you pass the last gas station, thronged with long-distance taxi drivers, moneychangers, *awalé*-players,[6] and cigarette women, you leave the asphalt behind to turn south on a rutted dirt road. Emerging from the last suburbs of the capital, the track runs through villages that become few and far between, past schools and churches perched on hillocks that shrink away as the miles go by.

The grayish-yellow road gradually turns ocher, then enters landscapes tinted saffron, crimson, or purple at the whim of the changing sunlight. Far from the dazzling green of the tea hills of Cyangugu and the luxuriant verdure of Kibuye's tropical forests, the road winds through hills and valleys of clay and dusty scrub. Fields of beans and yams alternate with raggedy-leafed banana groves. You brake for herds of nonchalant cattle, prodded by kids who don't even come up to their rumps; pass processions of women walking with basins of manioc on their heads and babies slung on their backs; encounter the odd van and minibuses called

Dubais, their shock absorbers sagging beneath the overload of passengers.

At the end of a footbridge spanning the muddy waters of the Nyabarongo River, a group of travelers sit slumped on cloth bundles, waiting for rides from the passing vehicles. On both sides of the bridge, as far as the eye can see, myriads of sacred ibises peck among the purple gallinules and pin-tailed black sand grouse floating amid the reeds. Beyond stretches the Bugesera, and here begins the district of Nyamata.

The area is bordered by three marshland waterways: to the north and east, the Nyabarongo, flanked by the bogs of Butamwa; on the west, the Akanyaru River, running through the swamps of Nyamwiza; to the south, Lake Cyohoha and the Murago Marshes. These muddy valleys, carpeted with papyrus and giant water lilies, crisscross the fifteen hills of Nyamata.

At the entrance to the commune, a cord stretched across the road marks the military checkpoint. The road then moves off into a landscape of red and green: the red-ocher of laterite that from now on will cling to skin, clothing, and floors; the pale green of banana farms, papyrus, shrubs, and brushwood. The houses of the first village you come to, Kanzenze, are of rammed clay and sheet metal. Across from two warehouses, three *cabarets*—which are the Rwandan equivalent of the Ivoirian *maquis* or the *terrasses* of Congo—form the heart of local public life.

On the right, a barely passable road climbs through an acacia forest to the heights of Kibungo. Farther along, a path descends toward the school in Cyugaro, which will be mentioned often in these accounts as a place of refuge. Going lower still, the track reaches the Nyamwiza Marshes described by Jeannette. Parakeets and West African gray parrots with hooked beaks call to one another among the foliage.

The village of Kibungo has not welcomed a car in ages. The deputy public prosecutor, the local councilman, and the district secretary of the department of education go there on their official motorcycles. A few shopkeepers, stock breeders, the primary school principal and teachers ride bicycles, which are usually laden with crates and jerry cans. Everyone else—women returning from the market, teenagers let out of school, members of the parish choir, farmers going to sell a goat or a sack of produce—walks through the forest in an endless column. At one last fork, those on foot scale a shortcut up a dry stone stream bed and rejoin the cyclists at the first adobe houses.

In the village square, a woman is sitting on a bench, leaning back against her house. Her name is Francine Niyitegeka. She smiles and introduces her infant, Bonfils, cradled in her arms. Her niece, Clémentine, is at her side. Francine is wearing a green floral pagne and a matching turban around her hair. Even from a distance, her beauty is remarkable, and looking closer, you see that her every gesture is imbued with exquisite grace. She is preparing to walk to the health center, twelve or thirteen miles away, because her baby is suffering from a brutal attack of malaria. The appearance of a foreign automobile, an unexpected godsend on this torrid afternoon, prompts her to overcome her shyness. She laughs and, like a good African, trades the initial interview for a round-trip by car to the clinic. On the first day she evokes her memories in snatches, sparingly, describing tragedy with delicate ellipses. As the interviews progress, her wariness vanishes; often she even becomes chatty, and at times quite merry.

FRANCINE NIYITEGEKA,
25 Years Old, Farmer and Shopkeeper
Kibungo Hill

The year of Independence, my parents were driven from their birthplace when a Belgian government truck brought them to the hill of Kibungo to clear a section of bush. Here, we never sincerely mixed with the Hutus nearby. People lived among their own ethnic group; no one quarreled with anybody. There were many inequalities in our dealings together, yet we did have an understanding.

A month or two before the genocide, however, alarming news of massacres began to spread through our neighborhoods. Behind our backs Hutu neighbors were yelling, "The Tutsis, those Tutsis, they absolutely must die!" And they spat other threats like that at us. New faces were appearing among the houses, and we would hear the *interahamwe* training in the forest, shouting encouragement to one another.

The *interahamwe* began to hunt Tutsis on our hill on April 10. Since they had never gone so far as to kill families in the churches, that same day we moved out in a long procession to seek refuge in the church in N'tarama. We waited five days.

As our brethren continued to gather, we became a great crowd. When the attack began, an onslaught of noise confused the full picture of the massacre, but I did recognize many faces of neighbors who were killing nonstop. Very soon I felt a blow: I fell between two benches, with chaos all around. When I woke up, I checked to be sure I was not dying. I made my way through the bodies, then escaped into the bush. Among the trees, I came upon a band of fugitives and we ran all the way to the marshes. I was to remain there for one month.

Then we lived out days beyond misery. Each morning we went to hide the littlest ones beneath the swamp papyrus; then we would sit on the dry grass and try to talk calmly together. When we heard the *interahamwe* arrive, we ran to spread ourselves out in silence, in the thickest foliage, sinking deep into the mud. In the evening, when the killers had finished work and gone home, those who were not dead emerged from the marsh. The wounded simply lay down on the oozing bank of the bog, or in the forest. Those who still could went up to the school in Cyugaro, to doze off in a dry place.

And in the morning, quite early, we'd trudge down to go back into the marshes, covering the weakest among us with leaves to help them hide. Out in the swamp, we came upon many naked women, because the Hutus stripped their dead victims of any pagnes in good condition. Truly, such sights spilled angry tears from our eyes.

I had found my fiancé again. Théophile and I would glimpse each other on the paths; we were sometimes together, but we no longer lived with any intimacy. We felt too shattered to find real words to say or any gentle ways to touch one another. I mean that if we happened to meet, it no longer much mattered, to either one of us, since more than anything else, we were both just trying to save our own lives.

One day, I got caught in my watery hiding place. That morning I had run into the marsh behind an old woman I knew. We were crouching silently in the water. The killers discovered her first, and I saw them cut her without bothering to drag her from the bog. Then they searched the surrounding foliage with the utmost care, because they knew all too well that a woman never hid just by herself. They found me, holding my child in my arms. They slaughtered my child. I asked to go out onto the grass and not die in the filth of slime and blood where the old woman was already lying. There were two men; I have not forgotten one feature of their faces. They dragged me into the papyrus and clubbed me, laying me out straightaway with a first blow full on the forehead, without cutting my throat. Often, they would leave the wounded in the mud for a day or two before returning to finish them off. As for me, though, I believe they simply forgot to come back there, that's why they botched the job.

I was unconscious for a long time. Then Théophile and some other fugitives found me near death and comforted me with a drink of water. I was no longer more than half alive, a prey to a bad fever and worse thoughts, but I was not afraid of death anymore. The wounds chose to spare my life, in any case, and I managed to get well on my own. In the evenings, Théophile tended me, fetching me handfuls of food from the fields. I finally brought myself back to life, returned to the business of survival, and rejoined my team. In the marshes, we tried to stay with the same group of acquaintants, to find easier comfort among ourselves. If too many people died, though, you'd have to find a new team.

During the evening gatherings, we heard no news from anywhere because the radios had stopped working, except in the killers' houses. Still, we did understand through hearsay that the genocide had spread throughout the country, that all Tutsis were suffering the same fate, that no one would come to save us anymore. We thought we were all doomed. Me, I now worried not about when I would die—since die we would—but about how the blows would slice into me and for how long, because I was terrified of the agony machetes cause.

I heard later that a small number of people committed suicide. Especially women, who would feel their strength fail and preferred the rushing river to getting hacked up alive. Choosing this death demanded too desperate a madness, because along the path that led to the Nyabarongo River there was an even greater risk of being caught by machetes.

On the day of the liberation, when the *inkotanyi* of the RPF[7] came down to the edge of the marshes and shouted that we could come out, no one wanted to move from beneath the papyruses anymore. The *inkotanyi* yelled their lungs out trying to reassure us, while we stayed under the leaves without a word. I personally think that at that moment, we survivors did not trust a single human being on this earth.

As for the *inkotanyi*, when they saw us finally creep out like mud beggars, they were stunned as we passed by. Most of all, they seemed bewildered, as though they were wondering if we were actually still human after all that time in the marsh. They were quite disturbed by our gauntness and stench. It was a disgusting situation, but they tried to show us the utmost respect. Some chose to line up in ranks, standing at attention in their uniforms, their eyes fixed upon us. Others decided to come over to support the weakest survivors. The *inkotanyi* were clearly having trouble believing all this. They wanted to appear sympathetic, but they hardly dared whisper to us, as though we could no longer truly understand reality. Except, of course, for some gentle words of encouragement.

Four months after the genocide, I married Théophile. We behaved as if nothing had changed between us, despite what had happened. And that's how we came back, saying softly what had to be said softly, and loudly what was to be said loud and clear. We live in a three-room *terre-tôle* house with our two little children and four orphans. The orphans, there's no point anymore in teaching them about the genocide —they've seen the worst of the real thing. My two young children, they'll learn the vital truth about the genocide later on. In any case, I think that from now on a gulf in understanding will lie between those who lay down in the marshes and those who never did. Between you and me, for example.

We talk with our neighbors almost every day about the killings, otherwise we dream of them at night. Talking doesn't soothe our hearts, because words cannot return us to times gone by, but keeping quiet encourages fear, withdrawal, and suchlike feelings of mistrust. Sometimes we joke about all that, we laugh, and yet we come back, in the end, to those fatal moments.

Myself, I don't wish to cry vengeance, but I hope that justice will offer us our share of peace of mind. What the Hutus did is unthinkable, especially for us, their neighbors. Hutus have always imagined that Tutsis were haughtier and more polished in their manners, but that's plain silly. Tutsis simply behave more temperately, in good times and bad. They are just more reserved by nature. It is also true that Tutsis prepare better for the future, it's part of their tradition. But in any case, in the Bugesera, Tutsis have never harmed Hutus. They haven't ever even spoken slightingly about them. The Tutsis were just as poor on the hills, they did not have larger properties, or better health and education than the Hutus.

I don't know if it makes any difference to say that now. I do it with some misgiving, because too many people are no longer here to speak for themselves, while fate has loaned me the opportunity to speak in my own voice.

Hutus still suffer from a bad idea of Tutsis. The truth is, it's our physiognomy that is the root of the problem: our longer muscles, our more delicate features, our proud carriage. That is all I can think of—the imposing appearance that is our birthright.

What the Hutus did, it's more than wickedness, more than punishment, more than savagery. I don't know how to be more precise, because although you can discuss an extermination, you cannot explain it in an acceptable way, even among those who lived through it. New questions always come at you out of nowhere.

My family is dead, and because of my headaches, I can no longer farm out in the sun. Since I was ready to go, I don't know why God chose for me not to die, and I thank Him. But I think of all those who were killed, and those who did the killing. I tell myself, the first genocide, I didn't believe it possible, so, regarding the likelihood of another one, I have no answer. Frankly, I expect that the suppressions of Tutsis are over for our generation; as to afterward, no one can predict our future. I know that many Hutus criticized those massacres, which they blamed as obligations. I see some Hutus who lower eyes weighed down by guilt. But I cannot glimpse much goodness in the hearts of those who are returning to the hills, and I hear no one asking for forgiveness. In any case, I know there is nothing that can be forgiven.

Sometimes, when I sit alone on a chair on my veranda, I imagine a possibility. If, on some distant day, a local man comes slowly up to me and says, "*Bonjour*, Francine. *Bonjour* to your family. I have come to speak to you. So here it is: I am the one who cut your mama and your little sisters," or, "I am the one who tried to kill you in the swamp, and I want to ask for your forgiveness," then, to that particular person, I could reply nothing good. A man, if he has drunk one Primus beer too many and he beats his wife, he can ask to be forgiven. But if he has worked at killing for a whole month, even on Sundays, how can he hope for pardon?

We must simply take up life again, since life has so decided. Thornbushes must not invade the farms; teachers must return to their school blackboards; doctors must care for the sick in the health clinics. There must be strong new cattle, fabrics of all kinds, sacks of beans in the markets. In that case, many Hutus are necessary. One cannot line up all the killers in the same row. Those who were overwhelmed by events, they can come back from Congo and the prisons one day, and return to their farm plots. We will begin to draw water together again, to exchange neighborly words, to sell grain to one another. In twenty years, fifty years, there will perhaps be boys and girls who will learn about the genocide in books. For us, however, it is impossible to forgive.

When you have lived a waking nightmare for real, you no longer sort through your daytime and nighttime thoughts the way you did before. Since the genocide, I always feel hunted, day and night. In my bed, I turn away from the shadows; on a path, I glance back at forms following me. When I meet a stranger's eyes, I fear for my child. Sometimes I see the face of an *interahamwe* down by the river and tell myself, Look, Francine, that man—you've seen him before in a dream . . . and I remember only afterward that this dream was that time, wide awake, back in the marshes.

I think that for me it will never end, being despised for my Tutsi blood. I recall my parents, who always felt persecuted in Ruhengeri. I endure a kind of shame over feeling hunted like that a whole life long, just because of what I am. The moment my eyes close upon that, I weep inside, from misery and humiliation.

KIBUNGO HILL

Francine is the wife of Théophile Mpilimba, the head local councilman in Kibungo, where she runs the village *cabaret*-bar —an establishment so modest that it has no sign—in a small house adjoining her own. The *cabaret* walls are of clay and straw, the floor of beaten earth, and there is one tiny window. In the back, cases of Primus beer contend for space with sacks of potatoes or beans and bottles of oil. There are benches along the walls where patrons can sit when it rains; in good weather, stools await them just outside the door. The usual drink is *urwagwa*, a strong, tart banana beer, or *ikigage*, a less tasty beer made from sorghum. The receptacles for these beverages are lined up behind the bar.

Banana beer is made without a still, according to a time-honored recipe. Bananas are buried for three days in a pit to become overripe; the juice is then pressed out and mixed with sorghum flour, which activates the fermentation that in four days produces an alcoholic drink somewhere between sweet wine and brandy. It must be drunk during the following week, before it inevitably turns too sour. The *urwagwa* of Kibungo was once the most famous in the region, and Kibungo was one of the most fertile hills, thanks to the alluvial soil along the river. That was before the genocide. One hillside belonged to the Tutsis, whose herds flourished on pastures descending all the way into the valley, and the other slope to the Hutus, who produced most of the alcohol and bean crop. Today these lands have lost two thirds of their men, the rare livestock are scattered among the bushes, and Francine often has no alcohol to sell.

The village sprawls over a flat area at the summit of the hill. At the entrance to Kibungo, brick buildings—a small church, a few schools, the town hall—encircle some magnificent *umuniyinya*, palaver trees in whose shade people are invited to sit during public assemblies or civic announcements. Other *umuniyinya* on the outskirts of the village are more commonly patronized by people taking naps.

On the town square, dashing among the houses and jockeying with goats for space on the grass, a swarm of scamps playing soccer kicks around a ball of foam-rubber tied up with strings. No dogs lounge around the gardens, the war having killed them or driven them all off in packs, and the few chickens are preyed on by feral cats. The path leaving the village descends to the river, passing cattle pens made of tree trunks bound together with vines and Hutu hamlets whose inhabitants (aside from the kids) no longer visit the village, except to sell their *urwagwa*.

Denise, an eighteen-year-old Hutu, lives in a house near the river with her sister Jacqueline, two little brothers and sisters, and her baby. Her parents and four older brothers never returned from the exodus to Congo. Denise proves very hospitable and considerate. She talks about her happy adolescence on the hill, the choir, parties at school, boys. She touches on the sadness of her life now, how she became the "back-up" of her baby's father, a wealthier farmer who lives two hundred yards down the hill, because she could no longer hope to find a real husband. She sends the children to the communal school without accompanying them into the village, and goes every week through the forest to the market in Nyamata to sell fish.

The view from the yard around her house is a striking panorama of treetops and, in the valley, the verdant expanse of the Nyamwiza Marsh, the refuge described by Jeannette and Francine. In spite of this obvious proximity, Denise claims that she neither saw nor heard anything during the massacres, no longer remembers where her family was in April 1994, and has received no news of their exile. She withdraws into silence at the very mention of the genocide. All her Hutu women neighbors react in the same way.

At the far side of Denise's manioc field, the path plunges down to end at Akonakamashyoza, a small island of reeds and the mythological juncture of the Nyabarongo and Akanyaru rivers, over which glide slender black pirogues. It is there, fishermen claim, at the mingling of the two sacred tributaries of the White Nile, that during the reign of the Tutsi kings two processions were held on the day after the death of the reigning monarch: the procession of the Living King, the heir, walking in the sunlight, followed by the procession of the Mummy, the dead king, in the moonlight.

In mid-afternoon in Kibungo, when everyone returns from the fields, women go into the gardens to shell beans and keep an eye on the cooking pots and little kids. The men stride purposefully off to the *cabaret*. At Francine's place, there are few requests for commercially bottled beer because it is expensive. Patrons with reasonable funds buy a bottle of *urwagwa*, into which Francine pokes the stem of a reed. The men drink and pass the bottle around, along with cigarettes. The most impoverished customers go behind the bar to drink a swallow straight from the jerry can, with a longer straw, under Francine's benevolent eye.

Later, the lowing of cattle is heard at dusk. Among the cowherds who return and join the drinkers is a boy, Janvier Munyaneza. Janvier looks after his older brother's cows and those of a neighbor, which is why he has not gone back to school. After he has penned up the animals and picked off their ticks, he takes his place at the bar. He doesn't drink alcohol yet, and with a greedy smile, accepts the proffered Fanta soda pop. His shyness is typical of Rwandans. Sitting amid a group of teenagers and children, he watches the adults drink and tell their stories late into the night. There is a sadness in his eyes that never leaves him, a melancholy confirmed by the hesitation in his voice from the first moment he speaks.

JANVIER MUNYANEZA,

14 Years Old, Cowherd
Kiganna Hill (Kibungo)

In school, I'd never heard one ethnic reproach. We kicked the soccer ball around without any hassles among ourselves, whenever time gave us a little break. On April 10, after Mass, some neighboring Hutus came to our house near the river to order us out, because they wanted to take it over, although without killing us. We went up right away to Kibungo, to stay with Grandfather.

Soldiers arrived the next day. When my uncle tried to sneak off, he didn't get far. They shot him dead. So then we fled to the church at N'tarama: Papa, Mama, my eight brothers and sisters, Grandfather and Grandmother. The *interahamwe* prowled around in the little wood surrounding the church for three or four days. One morning, they entered in a group, behind some soldiers and local policemen. They made a rush and began hacking people up, indoors and out. Those who were slaughtered died without a word. All you could hear was the commotion of the attacks—we were almost paralyzed, caught up in the machetes and the yelling of

the attackers. We were already just about dead before the fatal blow.

My first sister asked a Hutu she knew to kill her without any suffering. He said yes, dragged her by an arm onto the grass, and struck her once with his club. But a close neighbor, called Hakizma, shouted that she was pregnant. He sliced open her belly with a knife, opened her up like a sack. That is what human eyes have seen and no mistake.

Picking my way through the bodies, I had bad luck: a boy managed to get me with his iron bar. I collapsed onto the corpses, I didn't move, I made deadman's eyes. At one point, I felt myself being lifted and thrown. Other people landed on me. By the time I heard the *interahamwe* leaders whistle the signal to leave, I was all covered with dead people.

It was toward evening that some brave Tutsis from our area, who had run off into the bush, came back to the church. Papa and my big brother untangled us from the heap, me and my last sister, who was all bloody and died a little later in Cyugaro. In the schoolhouse, folks put dressings of healing grasses on the wounded. In the morning, we all decided to hide in the marshes. That's what we did every day, for a month.

We'd go down very early. The little ones hid first; the grown-ups stood watch and talked about what was happening to us. They hid last, when the Hutus arrived. Then, it was killing all the day long. At the beginning, the Hutus tried tricks in the papyrus. For example they'd say, "I recognized you, you can come out," and the most innocent ones would get up and be massacred where they stood. Or the Hutus would follow the faint cries of tiny children, who couldn't stand the mud anymore.

When the hunters found rich people, they would take them away to make them show where they'd hidden their money. Sometimes the killers would wait to collect a large group, to cut them all together. Or they'd gather a whole family so they could cut them in front of one another, and that spilled a big pool of blood in the marsh. Those still alive would go later to identify those who had been unlucky, by looking at the bodies in the puddles.

In the evenings, people would seek company in Cyugaro by acquaintance: neighbors together, young people together. . . . At first, small groups gathered to pray. Even folks who had never had a long habit of prayers, it seemed to comfort them to believe nevertheless in a little invisible something. But later on, they lost strength or faith, or they simply forgot, so no one bothered with that anymore.

The oldsters liked to go off to one side to talk over what was happening. There were some young people who would bring them small amounts of food that were just enough. But certain elders had no more children to help them. Every evening, they felt a growing collapse, because they no longer had the energy to dig in the ground and get by. Given their great age, they had too much pride to beg. So, one evening, they would say, "Well, now I'm not good for anything, tomorrow I'm not going down into the marsh." That's how many let themselves perish, sitting at dawn against a tree, without fighting back until the end of their old age.

On certain evenings, when the evildoers had not killed too much during the day, we would gather around glowing embers to eat something cooked; on other evenings, we were too downhearted. In the marsh, the next day at sunrise, we'd find the same blood in the mud, corpses rotting in the same places. The criminals preferred to kill the most people possible without bothering with burial. They must have thought they had all the time in the world, or that they weren't burdened with that stinking chore because they had already done their job. They also thought that those filthy bodies in the muck would discourage us from going to ground. We did try, though, to bury a few dead relatives, but it was rarely possible, we never had enough time. Even those animals that could eat them had run away from the tumult of the killings.

Those corpses bothered us so much that even among ourselves, we dared not speak of them. They showed us too harshly how our lives would end. I'm trying to say that their decay made our deaths more brutal. Reason why, every morning, our dearest wish was simply to make it one more time to the end of the afternoon.

When the *inkotanyi* came down to the marshes, to tell us that the massacres were over, that we would live, we didn't want to believe them. Even the weakest refused to leave the papyrus. Without a word, the *inkotanyi* went back the way they had come. They returned with a boy from N'tarama, who began yelling, "It's true! They're the *inkotanyi*, it's the RPF! The *interahamwe* are running off in a panic! Come out, you won't be killed anymore. . . ." We stood up. We saw one another on our feet, all of us in the middle of the afternoon, for the first time in a month.

At the assembly, a soldier explained to us in Swahili: "Now you are safe; you need to lay down your knives and machetes here. You don't need them anymore." One of us answered, "Machetes? We've had none since the beginning. All we have on our bodies is sickness, and we cannot lay that down. Even clothes—we haven't any others." Me, I was wearing only a torn pair of shorts, the same ones from the first day.

We left the worst-off survivors in the shade, so as to fetch them later in vehicles. We were escorted to Nyamata. After waiting a few days, my big brother and I went home to our land in Kiganna. Since our parents' house had collapsed, we moved here, to Kibungo, to the home of the grandfather who had been killed in the meantime. Anyway, it was too heavy a burden to live beside the river where we had been happy as a family.

Papa had twenty-four cows and five goats. We caught three cows in the bush, thanks to their distinctive patches of color. I live now with my big brother, Vincent Yambabaliye. I prepare his bowl for him morning and evening, I herd our cows and three others belonging to neighbors, out in the bush, while he farms our property. I don't like to go down into the valley, because I'm afraid the cows might trot off to the herds of the shopkeepers of Nyamata. We no longer have enough cattle to gather them around a paid cowherd. That's what is stopping my return to education, and every day it makes me sad.

In Kibungo, I have brought myself more or less back to life, but the sorrow of losing my family always takes me by surprise. I live too desolate a life. Off with the cows, I'm afraid of the rustlings in the bush. I would like to go back to the school-bench and begin learning again so that I could see something of a future for myself.

In Kibungo, when evening comes, it's clear that life has broken down. Many men wait impatiently to drink their Primus or *urwagwa*, our banana beer. They drink, and they no longer think about anything interesting: they say silly things, or nothing at all. As if they wanted only to drink on behalf of those who were killed, those who can't drink their share with them anymore, those whom, above all, no one wants to forget.

The genocide in Kibungo—we won't forget one scrap of its truth, because we share our memories. In the evening we often talk about this, we go over details with one another and try to be precise. Some days, we recall the most distressing moments, the sinister *interahamwe*; other days, we recall calmer times, when they had taken time off from our side of the marsh. We poke fun at one another, and then right away we go back to the most painful scenes.

Still, over time, I do feel that my mind sorts through my memories as it pleases, and I can do nothing about that. Same thing for us all. Certain episodes are much retold, so they swell with all the additions from one or another of us. Such episodes remain transparent, so to speak, as though they had happened yesterday or only last year. Other scenes are neglected, and they darken as in a dream. I would say that certain memories are perfected, and others are abandoned. But I know that we remember better now than before what happened to us personally. We're no longer interested in inventing, or exaggerating, or concealing, as at the liberation, because we aren't dazed anymore by fear of the machetes. Many people are less terrified or undone by what they have experienced. Sometimes we do talk overmuch among ourselves, and I get scared when I lie down in my bed.

When I pass the church in N'tarama, I look the other way going by the railings, and I avoid the hut of the Memorial. I don't want to see the rows of nameless skulls that may be my family's bones. Sometimes I go down to the edge of the marsh, I sit on a tussock of grass, and I look at the papyrus. Then, I see the *interahamwe* again, chopping with their machetes at whatever they found during the day. This awakens a sadness in me, and foreboding, but no hatred.

To feel hate, you must be able to direct it at definite names and faces. For example, those you recognized when they were killing—they must be cursed in person. But in the marshes, the killers worked in columns, we almost never made out their faces from beneath our leaves. Me, in any case, I can no longer imagine recognizable features. Even the face of my sister's murderer, I've forgotten it. I believe that hatred goes to waste against a mob of strangers. It's the opposite for fear. In a way, that's what I feel.

If I try to find a reason for this butchery, if I try to understand why we had to be cut, my mind takes a beating, and I waver in doubt over everything around me. I will never figure out the thinking of the Hutus who lived with us. Even the thoughts of those who did not strike us down directly, but said nothing. Those people wanted to hasten our deaths to take over everything. I see only greed and brute force as the roots of that evil.

I cannot grasp why our ethnic group is accursed. If I were not stopped short by poverty, I would travel far from here, to a country where I would go to school all week long, and play soccer on a nice grassy field, and where no one would want to mistrust me and kill me, ever again.

Lyre-Shaped Horns

In the Bugesera, it is unthinkable to photograph a cow without serious discussion with the owner and a gift to the herdsman. And yet cattle are everywhere: in the bush, the forests, on the playing fields and school lawns, among the flower and kitchen gardens, in the middle of the street. In Rwanda, however, cattle are much more than livestock. As one of the countless old sayings goes, "The cow is the supreme gift."

A cow is a sentimental offering, a gesture of friendship, or a loan, a reward, a bribe, a dowry, an investment made by several families for their children's milk. Two cows make a herd. Above that, you never say the number aloud, because that brings bad luck. Often the breeders gather five, twenty, thirty animals in the care of a ragged cowherd, whose shabbiness protects them from envious eyes.

The Rwandan cow belongs to the Ankole breed, named after a region in Uganda where it has had a long history. Originating supposedly in Upper Tibet, the Ankole is said to have crossed Persia and Abyssinia, dispersing thence toward the African Great Lakes Region, then to Senegal and South Africa. European historians date its entry into Rwanda at the end of the twelfth century. Tribes of Hamite nomads, the Tutsis' ancestors, are said to have driven gigantic herds into the hills and valleys of the land, settling on the summits, thus dominating the Hutus down in their fields and the Twa pygmies in their forests. This thesis was revived by the theoreticians of the genocide in an attempt to legitimize the extermination of the Tutsis and the slaughter of their herds. Ideology aside, however, the thesis is contested by a growing number of African and European historians. Cave paintings at numerous prehistoric sites in the Great Lakes area (contemporaneous with Mesopotamian frescoes) attest in fact to the presence there of the cattle and their breeders even before the large Bantu and Sudanese migrations at the beginning of the Christian era.

Ankole cattle are of medium size, slender and well muscled. A slight neck hump is a characteristic inherited from the Longhorn Zebu. Its coat is usually a solid buff, or *tache-tache*: spotted white and gray, black, or brown. The Ankole cow is distinguished by its splendid lyre-shaped horns, strong and sharp. For centuries, moreover, the unique criterion for selection and breeding has been the beauty of the animal's horns—to the dismay of veterinarians, who try in vain to encourage crossbreeding with European specimens and the adoption of more nourishing fodder for the animals.

Semi-domestic, half-wild, the Ankole is neither a good dairy nor meat animal. Beef is rarely eaten in the Bugesera, for that matter, and when it is, it proves a disappointment, for the meat is stringy and tough, unlike the delicious skewers of goat broiled on village street corners. Rwandan cattle-breeders will not kill their animals or allow their bloodlines to degenerate. "A single cow brings as many obligations as a herd, and more than a daughter," goes another proverb. The breeders like to show off their beasts, give them away, and above all, increase their numbers.

Farmers born and bred, Hutus consider the raising of livestock an unwarranted luxury in an overpopulated country of arid hills. They disdain cattle all the more in that before Rwanda became a republic, these animals symbolized the royal power of the Tutsi kings, who during celebrations would proudly spend whole days parading vast herds of cattle, their horns gleaming with grease, the way other rulers parade their tanks.

That explains why, from the first days of the genocide in the Bugesera, the *interahamwe* butchered the cows of their victims. To eat them, and to wipe them out. Many Hutus have now disclosed that the murderers would cut the animals' throats before their owners' eyes, to humiliate the Tutsis before killing them in turn. Hutu witnesses also speak at times of gargantuan barbecues on the evenings after huge slaughters. In the Bugesera, and throughout Rwanda, two thirds of the cattle population were destroyed during the killing, but their numbers have since rebounded. The survivors' insistence on rounding up the strayed cows, bringing new ones in from Uganda and Burundi, breeding them, reintroducing them to the deserted hilltops, and offering them to friends left desperately lonely by the extermination of their families shows the vitality of this traditional occupation.

Many well-meaning ethnologists, foreign aid workers, and journalists play down the distinctive differences between

Tutsis and Hutus. The country people, however, like nothing more than to resemble the stereotype that foreigners have
of them. That's how it is with the Argentine gaucho, the
Provençal fishmonger, or the Tahitian *wahine*, and the Tutsi
cattleman is no exception. You will never see a Hutu farmer
walking with a long staff and wearing a felt hat, whereas you
will often notice a Tutsi colleague with his cattleman's accessories, and in the evening or on weekends, you would not
be surprised to see a school principal, business manager, shopkeeper, or doctor stride into a café with hat and staff, which
proclaim him the owner of a cow in a Tutsi herd.

Jean-Baptiste Munyankore, a most dignified gentleman
of about sixty, a teacher at the school in Cyugaro for twenty-
seven years, is much attached to this custom. He wears a
short-sleeved white shirt as he shows off his classroom, stroll-
ing among the impeccably smooth wooden desks, caressing
them like a proud vintner patting his barrels. He puts on a
jacket and tie before a school administrative meeting, but he
takes up his long breeder's staff before going off to the *cabaret* or down into the town on Saturday. Jean-Baptiste inspires
the respect due an elder, because he was part of the first wave
of pioneers, those who fled the massacres at the end of the
reign of the *mwamis*, the Tutsi kings.

60 Years Old, Teacher
Cyugaro Hill (N'tarama)

I was a young man when we were exiled to the Bugesera. That was in 1959: the last *mwami*, Mutara III, had just drawn his final breath, and Hutus had taken over all positions of authority after the first general elections in Rwanda. I had finished my studies at the famous Teacher's School in Zaza. I had found a job in the volcanic region of Birunga, but no sooner had I walked into my classroom than I was shoved out of it, and I began to worry about what I was hearing behind my back.

In December of that evil year, Bahutu extremists marked the doors of Batutsi homes with paint in broad daylight, and returned during the night to set them on fire. We had therefore taken refuge with neighbors at the Catholic mission, where no one dared come after us in those times. As the days passed, we became too numerous, crammed in shoulder to shoulder. The Belgians did try to help us, but their major concern was the lack of proper hygiene. So one morning, a Belgian administrator turned up and asked us to write a list

of the countries where we wished to go into exile. I myself had heard nothing good about foreign lands, I had no family in Burundi or Tanzania, so I wrote down my own country, Rwanda. Many of us had done the same thing. "Fine," the administrator concluded. "You'll go to the Bugesera, since it's uninhabited."

That region of the Bugesera, we knew it only by name. The authorities brought army trucks into the mission court-yard. I climbed into a *rubaho*, a dump-truck with a wooden body, along with my wife, my younger brother, and my grandma. We were allowed the clothes on our backs and nothing more: neither utensils, nor blankets, nor books. That is how we traveled nonstop through the night, without know-ing what awaited us. I never looked back down that road and I have never again set the smallest toe in the prefecture of my childhood. We had crossed the bridge at the Nyabarongo River at first light. In those days, it was only two tree trunks, a kind of log ferry that you pulled on a rope to cross over. More trucks were waiting for us on the other side.

We set eyes on a land covered with savannas and marshes: we were entering the Bugesera. I thought, They are dump-ing us here to abandon us alive in the arms of death. With-out exaggeration: the swarming tsetse flies darkened the brightness of the sky. I still believe the authorities assumed that those terrible tsetse would be the end of us. We saw not one living creature anywhere on the trail. Then the first straw huts appeared. The only wooden-plank lodgings in Nyamata were the mission office, the district courthouse, the ad-ministrator's home, and an army camp in the Gako Forest.

After a week, we teachers set out in a small group to re-connoiter. While we were crossing some vast savannas, we suddenly found ourselves staring at a herd of elephants. We about-faced and took to our heels, because until then we'd only been around chickens and goats.

Later, we happily learned that here and there, Batutsi cattlemen and Bahutu farmers were living quite properly as neighbors on some remote hills over by Burundi. We camped out for a year, sheltering in huts made from cardboard and sheet metal. Actually, we were nourishing a frail hope that the situation would calm down, and that we could return to our ancestral homes. Alas, Batutsi refugees and bad news arrived with increasing frequency from the other prefectures.

Since we were surviving despite our poverty, the local administration gave us permission in 1961 to disperse and to claim land in the bush, as part of the celebration of the first anniversary of the Republic. So we signed up on a list of re-cipients, and when someone's number hit the first line, he went off to choose his five acres, which he could clear for himself.

Life was hard. We had to rip out bushes and tall shrubs amid the dust, dig through a thick crust of earth with wooden tools, plant sorghum and banana trees, build huts of mud and palm leaves. We had to defend ourselves against wild animals with bows and spears, and sometimes staves. Near my land, my eyes have seen the lion, the leopard, the spotted hyena, and the buffalo. There was no spring, and our stomachs were not used to drinking the stagnant water of the marshes, so many of us died of typhoid, dysentery, or malaria. To survive, we had to callus up our hands on tool handles, toil end-lessly in the sun and rain, and bring ever more children into the world. Then, we began to gain a tiny foothold in the markets. Our meager crops were purchased for shops in Kigali; with our small savings, we were able to buy a few baby goats. Local Batutsis started to offer us cows, out of kindness or to wed our prettiest girls.

We had always grouped ourselves according to acquaintance. N'tarama Hill was inhabited by newcomers from Ruhengeri, and the opposite slope by those from Byumba, while those from Gitarama settled lower down. On the hills, we gathered in large families, meaning, to use your vocabulary, in tribes. With the passing years, when the arrivals of Bahutus later increased, they did the same on other hills, and we did not mix much because of the distances. The Bahutus began coming above all as a result of directives from the minister of agriculture, when important officials realized that the bush of the Bugesera was being populated and cultivated. It was in 1973 that the Bahutus became as numerous as the Batutsis. Those Bahutus were hard workers, tough, and some of them set themselves up with savings. We quickly came to an understanding because we needed their money and their strong arms. As fellow farmers, we hardly ever shared a beer, but we spoke freely to one another, with propriety. We came from the same agriculture: beans, manioc, bananas, yams, the use of hoes and machetes. The Bahutus were better planters. As for the Batutsis, they raised cows, unlike the Bahutus, who never had the patience for them.

Since there were not many schools open to Batutsis, due to the admissions quotas in each district, we teachers would have the pupils sit in a circle in the shade of tall leafy trees, and we would improvise lessons right there in the dust. In the Bugesera, the authorities and the administration were Bahutu, as were the soldiers, the mayors, and those who controlled the purse strings. So, as soon as a Batutsi caught on to some learning, he became an instructor and taught school to Batutsi children.

That is how we teachers became very poorly regarded by the authorities, who were clearly jealous. They did not dare silence us directly, but the moment any killings began, teachers appeared high on the list, on the pretext that they had ties to the *inkotanyi*. The *inkotanyi* were the Batutsi rebels, the underground force in Burundi that launched attacks on Rwanda. Whenever the *inkotanyi* attacked the Bahutus, the army would go kill Batutsis as a punishment.

That's how things were. They would kill, in order: the families of men who had joined up in Burundi; then teachers, for reasons I've already explained; finally, the well-off farmers, so as to distribute their lands and crops to the latest Bahutu arrivals. One year would be burning-hot; the next year, quite calm. For example, 1963 was a year when thousands were murdered, as a natural response to the many rebel expeditions. 1964 was a quiet year. 1967 was disastrous in the way of deaths: that year, soldiers threw hundreds of Tutsis alive into the Urwabaynanga, a great pool of oozing mud over by Burundi, where you can actually go fish out the proof. In 1973, they went as far as to kill students in their classrooms.

... The massacres were unpredictable. That's why, even when the situation seemed peaceful, both our eyes never slept at the same time.

And yet, we Batutsis, we had driven off the wild animals, conquered the tsetse, and learned to submit to the authorities. In spite of the ethnic friction, our villages were multiplying, Batutsis were holding their own in numbers against the Bahutu population, and their herds were increasing. Certain Batutsis were becoming a bit wealthy, with Bahutus beginning to work for them. Nyamata was growing fast; the shops were mixed, but the best-stocked ones were Batutsi. *Cabarets* were appearing, and immediately became quite popular. Life was hard, but did not seem too bad.

There were many excellent people among the Bahutus. I remember one day, I was already tied to a tree before a row of army guns, because I bore the tribal name of a rebel leader. The only thing left to do was die, but I kept proclaiming my innocence. A captain on inspection tour happened to notice me at death's door and shouted to the soldiers, "I know that man's voice: he is first-named Jean-Baptiste, from Cyugaro, he's a good teacher, he has nothing to do with the rebel commandos," and he had the ropes cut. Many Bahutus grew ever more suspicious of Batutsis, though, on account of the *inkotanyi*. And because decent farmland, well, there was less and less of it available.

This discord grew poisonous after the authorization of a multi-party electoral system in 1991. When meetings began, public discussion became too dangerous; the exchange would boil up quickly, with the risk of injury every time. *Interahamwe* arrived to parade along the roads and paths, and they swaggered around in the *cabarets*. The radio called the Batutsis cockroaches; Bahutu politicians predicted at gatherings that the Batutsis would die. They were dreadfully afraid of the *inkotanyi* and a foreign military invasion. I believe that was when they began to think about the genocide.

In 1992, the tally of Batutsi corpses in the forest came to four hundred without the slightest protest from the chief of police. When the war broke out two years later, we were already accustomed to killings. I myself anticipated the usual tragedy, nothing more. I thought, Things are too hot to take the main road, but if we don't go down off the hill, we might manage. After the massacre in the church, I realized that our plight had become deadly. That day, I joined the stream of fugitives flowing down to the Nyamwiza Marsh to crouch in the mud.

In the beginning, deep in the papyrus, we hoped help would come. But God Himself showed that He had forgotten us, so all the more reason for the Whites to do the same. Later, each day we hoped only to make it to the next dawn. Down in the marshes, I saw ladies crawling through the mud without a whimper. I saw a nursling sleeping forgotten on his mama, who had been cut down. I heard people with no muscle strength to walk at all announce their longing to eat some corn, one last time. Because they knew perfectly well that they would be dispatched the next day. I saw the skin fold into wrinkles on people's bones, week after week. I heard songs tenderly hummed to comfort the moans of death.

In the forest, I happened upon the news of the death of my brother's two children, who had passed the national university entrance exam. In the swamp, I learned of the deaths of my wife, Domine Kabanyana, and of my son, Jean-Sauveur. My second son died behind me while we were running through the marsh. We'd been trapped by a surprise attack, but had tried to escape our pursuers anyway. His flight ended when he stumbled over a tussock of thornbushes; he cried out one word, I heard the first blows, I was already far away. . . . He was in the fourth grade.

You must understand that we fugitives, although we lived "all for all" in our evening camp, were forced to live "everyone for himself" during our flights through the swamp. Except, of course, for the mamas carrying their little ones.

In the evening, four families gathered in my house in Cyugaro. We no longer spread mats and mattresses on the floor because the *interahamwe* had stolen them. We engaged in a little conversation, especially details about the day's happenings or words of comfort. We did not argue, we teased no one, we did not mock the women who had been raped, because all the women expected to be raped. We were fleeing the same death, we endured the same fate. Even former enemies no longer found a reason to quarrel, because there was just no point in that anymore.

We would talk a bit, in those days, about the why of that damned situation, and we would come up against the same answers. The Bugesera, once deserted, had become crowded. The authorities were scared of being hunted down by the "Ugandans' RPF." The Bahutus were making eyes at our lands. . . . But all that did not explain the extermination, and still doesn't today.

I personally can point to an historical anomaly. The history books about the Belgian colonization taught us that the Batwa pygmies with their bows were the first inhabitants of Rwanda. Then the Bahutus arrived, with hoes. The Batutsis followed with their cattle, acquiring too much land because of their vast herds. But here, in our region of the Bugesera, the arrivals occurred in precisely the opposite order, since the Batutsis came first, clearing the land as pioneers, bringing nothing in their hands. And yet, the genocide in the Bugesera was just as efficient as it was everywhere else. Therefore, I refute those historical explanations. I think that the history dictated by the colonial authorities programmed the Bahutu yoke set upon the Tutsis—a program that through bad luck, if I may put it that way, turned into genocide.

Today I suffer from poverty in many ways. My wife is dead and I have lost everyone in my family except two children. I had six cows, ten goats, thirty hens; now my yard is empty. My close neighbor is dead; the man who offered me my first cow is dead. Out of the nine teachers in the school, six were killed, two are in prison. After such long years, becoming a true friend to new colleagues is a trying and awkward thing, when one has lost the familiar people of the past. I married again, to one of my wife's younger sisters, but I live a life that no longer interests me. At night, I traverse an existence all too crowded with my dead relatives, murder victims who all talk among themselves but ignore me, not even bothering to look at me anymore. By day, I suffer from a different kind of loneliness.

What happened in Nyamata, in the churches, in the marshes and on the hills, were the abnormal actions of perfectly normal people. Here's why I say that. The principal and the inspector of schools in my district joined in the killings with nail-studded clubs. Two teachers, colleagues with whom I used to share beers and student evaluations, pitched in to help, so to speak. A priest, the mayor, the assistant chief of police, a doctor—they all killed with their own hands.

These intellectuals had not lived at the time of the Batutsi kings. They had not been robbed or victimized in any way, they were under no one's obligation. They wore pressed cotton trousers, they had no trouble sleeping, they traveled around in cars or on mopeds. Their wives wore jewelry and knew city manners, their children attended white schools.

These well-educated people were calm, clearheaded, and they rolled up their sleeves to get a good grip on their machetes. So, for someone who has taught the humanities his whole life long, as I have, such criminals are a fearsome mystery indeed.

At the Widows' Corner

The primary school in Cyugaro, rebuilt in brick, today houses twenty-five classes in which Tutsi and Hutu children share the same benches. In the village, most of the mud houses are cracking or collapsing, and weeds are invading the gardens. The school is three miles from the marshes. The only path crosses fields of manioc and runs past the walls of two burned-out houses. Yellow-flowering *iwuwa* and red-flowering *umuko* trees embellish the savanna, through which roam bands of children hunting for wild cabbages. Then the trail plunges into a eucalyptus forest that glows with light filtering through the tall trees.

The vast green plain reappears on the other side of the forest. The path descends abruptly to an edging of wild banana plants, beyond which lie the marshes. The first impression is of an impenetrable entanglement of waterlogged reeds and papyrus, yet it is possible to enter this mass by moving the mats of stems aside with both hands. Spongy in the dry season and muddy in the wet, the ground smells of putrid sludge. Each step sinks calf-deep. The buzzing of flies, mosquitoes, and dragonflies provides a background to the melodious laughter of ibises and the shrill cries of macaques and bands of playful black talapoins, small monkeys whose watery acrobatics can just be glimpsed. If you don't move, and remain patient, you may also hear the grunting of unseen wild pigs, or the rustle of tall grasses at the passage of slender marsh antelopes called sitatungas.[8]

Leaving the marsh, we meet a boy of about fifteen, his back bent under a load of peat, which is burned for fuel. Every afternoon, he burrows into the marsh for hours to hunt waterfowl or collect peat. He invites us to his adobe house, which sits in an enclosure of palms high on a butte, overlooking the expanse of papyrus. His name is Jean-Claude Khadafi. He offers us *urwagwa* in wooden bowls, checks his banana pit, sits down by its edge, and talks about the genocide. During that time, his home sheltered elderly fugitives too weak to climb the slope all the way to the school, and who would sometimes give up hiding in the mud to spend one last day under a roof, waiting for the inevitable killers to come finish them off. Many people have thus become memories for Jean-Claude.

Today, he lives with the only other survivor of their family, his father, who left this morning at dawn to roam the forest until evening, when he will return without a word, as he does every day. Jean-Claude prefers the isolation of his home, between the eucalyptus and the papyrus, to lodgings in a new house in the Nelson Mandela projects farther up the path, closer to the schools and his pals. He explains that not a day goes by that he doesn't visit the marsh, that neither the sultry dog-days nor bouts of malaria could keep him away.

And his gaze does seem never to stray for long from the flat green surface of the strangely whispering foliage.

From his house, a bush track leads to the junction at Kanzenze. Once the site of a lively market, that village is now a simple minibus stop. Just off the trail is Marie Mukarulinda's *cabaret*, once a popular venue for local wheelers and dealers. Like all public rooms, this one is painted a chipped and faded African green. The seats have seen better days; cases of Primus and Fanta sit stacked against the wall.

Marie is noticeably tall and slender. In the morning, she works in the fields; in the afternoon, she tries to keep her late husband's *cabaret* going, thanks to a managerial style of the utmost simplicity: whatever coins are occasionally received from a customer buying a beer serve immediately to provide a bottle to a regular fallen on hard times. Outside, the backyard is the smoky domain of another widow and Marie's inseparable accomplice: a large lady named Pétronille who prepares on her grill the most delicious goat brochettes in the entire Bugesera.

Marie's *cabaret* is called The Widows' Corner, because many local women, most of them widowed by the genocide, like to meet there and share a bottle or two of Primus, just to gossip up a storm and laugh at everything and nothing, and especially themselves. Today, for example, a veterinarian has come from Kigali to supervise the artificial insemination of a herd of goats. Invited to the *cabaret* after his visit, he is taken aside by Marie's friends, who insist that he must make a return visit to take care of *them*. Taken aback, he freezes . . . until a general outburst of laughter tells him he's been had, whereupon he makes amends for his gullibility by ordering drinks all around.

In one corner of the veranda, sitting stiffly on a stool a touch apart from the others, is a thin man carefully dressed in a threadbare and much-mended black double-breasted suit, his face impeccably shaved, his gray mustache neatly combed. He is Monsieur Gaspard. He is the neighborhood patriarch, whose distinction is equaled only by the concision of his eighty years of memories. Sole survivor of a family of twelve, Gaspard bears his solitude with dignity. With never a hint of complaint, he admits that he now lives with only sadness and poverty for company, simply waiting for the end of his life, in the chair in his hovel nearby or on a stool at Marie's *cabaret*, before a bottle of beer slipped to him discreetly by neighbors and which he savors very, very slowly. As a farewell, he quotes this Rwandan proverb in Kinyarwanda: *Amarira y'umugabo atemba ajya mu unda*, which means, "A man's tears flow in his belly."

In a clearing a mile or so away, off toward Nyamata, three houses of clay and straw sit by the path. Angélique Mukamanzi has been settled in one of them, the property of a Hutu peasant in exile, until her family home can be completely repaired. Angélique is a young woman who makes it a point of honor never to wear dresses or pagnes, but only black pants, "country" denim jackets, and "European" blouses. Coming back from the fields or the market, she hastens to touch up her nail polish, slip into leather sandals or pumps, and spend the day's end leaning against the wall of the house with her neighbors, as if she were passing time before her date showed up. She had recently acquired a suitor: handsome, attentive, and funny, an agronomist by profession. But, she says, with a somewhat ironic smile, she had felt obliged to break things off, once she realized he was a Hutu.

During the genocide, as the weeks went by in the marshes, she inherited a little band of orphans and became a kind of big sister or adoptive mother. Now, willy-nilly, she is the head of their family.

ANGÉLIQUE MUKAMANZI,
25 Years Old, Farmer
Rwankeli Hill (Musenyi)

With my sister Laetitia, I take care of eight children left on their own. It just happened naturally. In the marshes, when parents would go off into death without taking along their little ones, those who had none, like us, offered to take them on in the pinch. Later, time entrusted them to us for good.

Before the war, I studied hard, because I wanted to pass the national exam in Kigali and snag myself a fine career. Boys had a good eye for me, life seemed worthwhile. In school, I had mixed friends, Tutsi and Hutu. The latter never said bad things. I felt the first fears when people began leaving the Bugesera after the clashes in 1992. Our paths then grew loud with more and more evil words. That's another reason why I wanted to turn toward the capital.

Three days after the plane crash, a small group of us—my family and our neighbors, with bundles of belongings—moved into the church at N'tarama. During the day, the brave among us would venture into the nearby fields to bring back food. At night we slept inside or outdoors, depending on our strength. When the *interahamwe* surrounded the fences, some men began throwing small rocks to slow down their advance. The women gathered the stones, because they did not want to die just any old way, but this resistance was too weak. Grenades exploded against the front door. I myself was in the back: for an hour I ran so hard down the slope I don't remember breathing, until I plunged into the *urunfunzo* of the marshes, which I had heard about but never seen before. *Urunfunzo* are the papyrus plants. At the time, of course, I had no idea that for an entire month I would spend my days in the mud from head to toe, at the mercy of mosquitoes.

The killers worked in the marshes from nine to four, four-thirty, while the daylight lasted. Sometimes, if it was raining too heavily, they would come later in the morning. They arrived in columns, announcing themselves with whistles and songs. They would beat drums, seeming quite delighted to kill all day long. One morning, they would take one path, and another the next day. When we heard the first whistles, we'd dash in the opposite direction. One morning they cheated, coming from all sides to set traps and ambushes, and that day it was most disheartening, because we knew that come evening there would be so many more dead than usual.

In the afternoon they no longer sang, because they were tired, and they would set out for home, chatting as they went. They fortified themselves with drinks and ate the cattle, because they were slaughtering them along with the Tutsis. Truly, these killings were quite coolly done, and well-planned. If the liberators of the RPF had taken another week to arrive, not one Tutsi in the Bugesera would still be alive, to stand up to the lies—for example, about the supposed drunkenness of the criminals.

In the evening, after the killing, we would scatter into the night to dig in the fields, collecting manioc and beans. It was also banana season. We ate raw stuff for a month, with both hands—dirty hands, like human trash. It was the same fate for adults and little children, who no longer had a chance to drink their mother's milk or eat nourishing things. So, many people spared the machetes were overtaken by mortal weaknesses. In the morning, we would awaken and find them next to us, stiffened in their sleep. Without one word of farewell, without a last gift of time allowing us to cover them over with proper humanity.

On rainy nights, we seized the chance to rub ourselves with palm leaves, scraping off the thickest of our waste and the muddy filth. Then we would lie down on the ground. We talked over our day, wondering who had died this time, and who would die tomorrow. We spoke of the grim fate bowing us down. We could rarely find happy words to say, amid all our crushing sorrows.

In the morning, we could not even take a moment to dry off in the rising sun. Soaking wet, we'd set out to hide the children in small groups under the papyrus. We used to tell them to be as good as fish in ponds. In other words, to stay underwater up to their necks, and not to cry. We gave them the foul swamp water to drink, even if it was sometimes tinged with blood. And then we smeared ourselves with mud, too. Once in a while, we could just make one another out through the surrounding foliage. We asked ourselves why God was abandoning us there, among the snakes, which luckily did not bite anyone.

One night, my heart was struck a bloody wound that can never heal. Leaving my hiding place that evening, I saw that they had caught Mama. She lay floating in the mud. Her name was Marthe Nyirababji. Papa, and Godmother, and the whole family were killed not long afterward, on that terrible April 30. Papa's name was Ferdinand Mudelevu. He was pierced through by a Hutu neighbor who danced and sang over him. After that, I had to team up with other survivors from the hill. Through the papyrus branches, my eyes have looked into those of the *interahamwe* killing close by. I saw many people cut down beside me. That whole time I battled a devouring fear, a truly overpowering terror. I overcame it, but I am not saying that I have beaten it forever.

At the end of the genocide, I was placed for three months in an abandoned hut on a lower slope of Nyamata Hill. I should have been content, but I was still too anxious and exhausted. We felt like strangers in our own skins, if I may put it that way; we had been brought low, and were disturbed by what we had become. I think we didn't believe we would ever be truly safe again.

Deep down, we thought we would never be free of our past danger, and we waited weeks before allowing ourselves to taste happiness. I would walk an hour every day to get to our family property. I wielded the hoe to feed the children. I molded mud bricks to build a new house, with the help of a mason sent over by the district.

At present, while waiting for our roof to be laid on, I live in the house of a Hutu who has not returned from Congo. I base my hopes on a plan for a small business of rice, sugar, or salt on the main street near a pharmacy. You get used to work, but not regrets.

Before the war, I was too fond of school, and had decided to turn away from village life. If the genocide had not over-run us, I might have passed the national exam, I would have gotten my law degree and worn a lawyer's robes in a private practice in Kigali. But now I am twenty-five. I see only obstacles in my life, marshlands around my memories, and the hoe reaching its handle out to me. I no longer know where to turn to find a husband. I cannot put myself in the care of a Hutu man. I'm not necessarily hoping for a survivor. I have forgotten the fantasy of love. I'm waiting simply for the gentle eyes of an everyday man seeing me for who I am. I hear plenty of candidates knocking at the door and introducing them-selves in brushed-up shoes, but I see no one anymore, no matter where I look, who could provide me with tenderness.

Many Hutu families came back to the hills, even when their men were in prison. The authorities hold the doors of their homes wide open to them. Some people did not agree at all with what was happening, while others supported it completely. These families farm their fields among them-selves, they return nothing that they looted, they hardly speak to us, they seek no forgiveness. Their silence upsets me deeply. I'm certain that I have recognized the faces of a few criminals among these families, when they are out on their land. Their arms are still well-muscled for farmwork. My sister and I have only thin arms to feed the children left on their own. I do not find it fitting to entrust the difficult task of reconciliation simply to time and silence.

In N'tarama, some survivors go bad or give up hope. They say, "I had a strong husband, I had a house with stout walls, I had lovely children, I had big cows, I worked every day and every tomorrow, and all that for nothing." There are many men and women who no longer make an effort. Once they get their hands on some small change, they drink Primus, and they don't give spit for anything. They get drunk on alcohol and bad memories. Some take pleasure in always talking about the same deadly moments they once lived through. As if they could not do without that anymore.

Me, when I listen to them, I understand that as time goes by, people do not remember the genocide in the same way. For example, a neighbor woman tells how her mama died in the church; then, two years later, she explains that her mama died in the marsh. To me, there is no lie. The daughter had an acceptable reason to first want her mama's death at the church. Maybe because she had abandoned her while running through the marsh and felt bad about that. Maybe because it was a comfort to her in unbearable distress, to convince herself that her mama had suffered less that way, from one mortal blow on the first day. Afterward, time offered a little tranquility to that daughter, so that she could remember the truth, and she accepted it.

Another girl denies that she was wounded, even though her arms show obvious scars. But one day she will hear someone talk about an episode involving a trap for sex, and she, in turn, she will dare to talk about her own ambush and to what she owes the miracle of her life. She hasn't lied either: she has waited for a sympathetic audience familiar with misfortune before revealing a painful truth.

There are also people who constantly change the details of a fateful moment because they believe that on that day, their lives snatched away the luck of another life that was just as deserving. But in spite of these zigzags, a person's memories do not fade away, thanks to talking with others, in small gatherings. People choose certain memories, depending on their characters, and they relive them as if they had happened last year, and will go on for another hundred years.

Some people claim that the difference between Hutus and Tutsis is an invention. I cannot understand nonsense like that, because after the slaughter began in the Bugesera, no Tutsi could draw breath for a single hour standing out in the open among Hutus. But I don't want to go into anything about this difference and the so-called misunderstanding between the ethnic groups. I believe that we must be given an appropriate justice, but I don't want to say whether the prisoners ought to be shot. Neither do I wish to express what I think about why the Whites watched all these massacres with their arms crossed. I believe that Whites take advantage of quarrels among Blacks to sow their own ideas afterward, and that's all. I don't wish to say anything about what I glimpse in the hearts of Hutus.

I'm simply saying that Hutu compatriots agreed to exterminate Tutsi compatriots in the marshes so that they could loot their houses, ride on their bicycles, eat their cows.

From now on, I consider this desolate time that passes before me as an enemy. I suffer from being tied to this present life, which is not the one I was supposed to have. Among neighbors, when we ask ourselves why the genocide chose the little spot of Rwanda on the map of Africa, we get lost in discussions that tangle up and never lead to any answers that can fit together.

Bicycle-Taxis Under an Acacia

A service station, the hangout of the tire-repair men, marks the beginning of Nyamata's main street. Much wider and redder than the track it prolongs, the main street is stony and potholed along the side used by vehicles, sandy along the side used by pedestrians. Across from the gas pumps, an empty lot serves as a station for trucks and "Dubai" minibuses, which park there long enough to change passengers, goats, and bundles.

Lined up at the top of the main street are the religious bookstore, the ruins of the Bugesera Club (haunt of the former soccer team), and Chez Clémentine, the first little hole-in-the-wall that serves banana beer. Taking any alleyway on the right, going past small courtyards and shanties swarming with kids, you will emerge almost immediately into the fields. If you take a street on the left, you'll find the Pentecostal church, where the open-air chorales—sophisticated, exuberant, sometimes hysterical—are astonishing musical events. Straight ahead takes you "downtown," to the marketplace.

The first two-story house in Nyamata, the project of a tradesman from Burundi, has not yet progressed beyond the foundations. The only private car left on the streets is a white Suzuki owned by another merchant. All destroyed now, or taken off into exile, the automobiles that once crowded the bustling little town have not been replaced. The few vehicles that do raise dust along the main street are shopkeepers' vans, which are sometimes requisitioned for processions at weddings, funerals, and sporting events, as are the all-terrain vehicles of the humanitarian organizations and the local administration. So the traffic consists of Japanese one-cylinder motorbikes, carts pulled by oxen outfitted with peculiar aluminum yokes, and of course, mostly bicycles and pedestrians.

The chief bicycle-taxi station is at a corner of the marketplace where, in the shade of a spreading acacia, thirty or so drivers await clients while listening to the radio. Off to one side, a shed serves as a workshop for bike mechanics—often just little kids—who repair crank gears and wheels with wizardly skill.

The bikes, all black, are mostly Boda-bodas[9] with wide rims and fat tires in various stages of baldness. The bikes are sometimes equipped with a front shock absorber and always have clamp brakes worked by levers set low on the frame. The comfortable leather saddles, perched upon three enormous springs, provide a gyroscopic suspension ideal for cushioning jarring rides over rough roads. Melodious bells are mounted on the handlebars and sparkling reflectors on the wheel spokes. As for the chrome-work and accessories, they depend on the model. Some bikes are decorated with gilt strips, others are protected by an umbrella or equipped with a seat over the front wheel. Some sport an anti-theft system, a vanity mirror, or a framed religious image. The luggage racks of the bikes are padded with a removable leather cushion to allow the transportation of either passengers or merchandise.

The other taxi stands are near the hospital, at the Tuesday cattle market, and at the English-language lycée when school lets out. The price of a ride in town ranges between three and five francs. The fare for longer trips through the forest is negotiated on the spot.

Errand boys and deliverymen also work on bikes. Messages, bags of flour, trunks, furniture, goats, jerry cans of gas—everything travels by bike. When night falls, at the hour of the twilight Primus, delivery guys shuttle among the warehouses and *cabarets*, ferrying on their luggage racks stacks of bottle crates secured via an infallible system of bungee cords.

Near the main street, in courtyards where pots of *fufu*—manioc paste—are simmering, two "theaters" identified by their posters show grainy videos with scratchy soundtracks on even hours only. The films of Jean-Claude Van Damme compete with the "Rambos" of Sylvester Stallone. Since the destruction of the dance halls, young people listen to music outside local hairdressing salons called One Love, Chez les Sportifs, and Texas. The main street also offers ten or so pharmacies, three or four photography studios, a health clinic, a bakery (Au Bon Pain Quotidien), a butcher's shop (Butcher), but no music store, no fashion shoppe, and even more surprising in an African town, no jewelry store.

The main street is hardly ever empty, welcoming officials and office workers on their noon break, taking on the colors of a whole slew of children after classes—the royal blue of schoolgirls' dresses, the khaki uniforms of schoolboys, the white shirts and blouses of older students—and on market days, blooming with the red, yellow, green, and blue panels of many parasols. Deserted for the kickoff of the soccer matches played on the field at its far end, the street fills up again at half-time. Making up for the lack of telephones, the main street is where people come to hear and spread the news about one and all.

Innocent Rwililiza, who dreads facing too many shadows at home, is one of the most popular fixtures on the main street. He knows everybody, thanks to ten years of school on the hills and fifteen of teaching in the town. He is the secretary of the school inspection board and the founder of several mutual aid associations. He is one of the twenty heroic survivors of Kayumba Forest. He belongs to no clan, but never fails to lend a hand. His criticism is always delivered gently, his ideas expressed with kindness. The one thing that makes him uneasy is any mention of the local church, where his first wife perished. Épiphanie, his second wife, has already given him four children.

He drinks only Primus—one, two, five bottles, depending on the company—and likes it lukewarm. Any other beer, or temperature (which he detects immediately by feeling the bottle), or any other beverage, for that matter, would make him immediately sick to his stomach. He is curious about everything, about foreigners and foreign countries, but he focuses his intelligence—hopelessly, he knows—on trying to fully grasp what he went through. One of his dreams is to write a book about the genocide, but he claims to have not yet found the time or energy for that. In the meantime he talks about the genocide, discusses it, jokes about it—a lot—with everyone, not only to understand better and forget nothing, but because talking does him some good.

INNOCENT RWILILIZA,

38 Years Old, Teacher
Nyamata Town Center

My father was an assistant veterinarian in Ruhengeri. He was sent off along with so many others to clear a patch of land for crops on Kanombe Hill. And that is what he did, with his own two hands. In Rwanda, agriculture is not something that can be taught: it comes to you. If you have nothing better to do for a while, you take your hoe and you go dig in the fields.

When my parents crossed the Nyabarongo River, the few native Hutus already living scattered out in the bush were not hostile at all. Those people knew nothing of the turmoil being plotted in the rest of the country, and they looked upon the refugees quite peacefully.

In Kanombe, we children were just two brothers and two sisters. We lived in a straw hut. It was over twelve miles on foot through the bush to go to school each day. Sundays were spent clearing land, of course. I went to primary school, then secondary school, and I became a teacher. I married and came down with my wife to live in the center of town in Nyamata, because the arable land on the hills was packed with people.

At that time, Nyamata already deserved to be called more than a village, with a worthy market and a church built to last. Houses had sprung up quickly, and the streets were much changed. One saw businesses of all kinds, a minibus station for Kigali, *cabarets* with local drinks or export beers, a secondary school, a very modest hotel, and a cultural center with a pretty lawn. Nyamata seemed well on the way to becoming a town; some people even spoke of a prefecture, despite the harsh threat of droughts. With a population that was slightly more Tutsi than Hutu, we felt comfortable here.

It was afterward, around 1992, that politics came to spoil everything. Militias and politicians arrived from Kigali to send ominous signals. One Hutu mayor was even killed because he refused to hunt down Tutsis. We no longer mixed much at all in the *cabarets*, for fear of injury, but we spoke correctly to one another at work and on the road. Like everyone else in 1994, I could smell catastrophe cooking on the coals. One no longer dared go into this or that *cabaret* without being a member of such and such a political party. We Tutsis, we simply chose Tutsi shops to drink our Primus without getting into trouble.

I remember one evening, a few weeks before the attacks, I was coming home from work with a Hutu colleague and neighbor. We were talking about the negotiations at the Arusha summit[10] between the government and the rebels, and about our political worries. Halfway up the slope, he stopped, looked at me, and said, "Innocent, your people will be wiped out." I replied, "No, I don't think so. Once again we will suffer, but we will surely save ourselves." Then he repeated, using the familiar tone of a friend, "Innocent, listen to me: I must tell you that you are all going to die." Later, I saw this colleague in the neighborhood, riding around in a van full of soldiers from the army camp at Gako, pointing out the doors of those who had to be killed. He saw me, and just got on with the job.

After Habyarimana's plane crashed, we continued to teach during the day, but at night we slept out in the bush, far from any houses, for fear of surprise attacks. On the morning of April 11, there was a great uproar in Nyamata: out in the streets, soldiers had begun shooting in earnest. Quickly realizing that the people posed no threat, however, they stopped using up cartridges and simply helped out the *interahamwe*, who had already swarmed there with clubs and machetes. They began with the prosperous businessmen, because even from the start they were preoccupied with getting rich.

In the panic, a crowd rushed to the town hall. We stayed in the courtyard there for about two hours, waiting for words of protection. When the mayor came out, wearing his official blue outfit, he told us, "If you go home, you will be killed. If you flee into the bush, you will be killed. If you remain here, you will be killed. You must leave here in any case, because I do not want any blood in front of my town hall." The women, children, and the weak or infirm started to walk to the church. Me, I thought, This business has taken a twist: they will kill there, too, that's for certain, and besides, I don't want to die in a church. Reason why I ran all day without any destination. I spent the night in the woods and reached

Kayumba the next day. There, we wound up some six thousand able-bodied people, about a mile and a half from Nyamata, waiting in the eucalyptus forest for whatever was to come.

From the top of Kayumba, we could see smoke and hear the grenades on the day of the massacre in the church. My wife and child had taken refuge inside. Four days later, I met a mama in the woods who had escaped the slaughter. She told me, "Innocent, I bring bad news: I saw your wife during the mêlée in the church. Given the state in which I left her, I must tell you that she is no longer of this world." I was shattered, but I yet had hope. I told myself, If no one has seen her body, perhaps she managed to escape, too.

Even today, years later, when I catch sight in the distance of a silhouette that resembles her, it still startles me. It is so draining to live with a false hope. I can now say that surviving with the memory of your wife and child, when you don't know how they were killed, when you have not seen them dead, and when you have not buried them, is what takes the most heart out of you.

I could not bring my wife and my son along with me to Kayumba Hill because they could not run fast enough. I did not follow them to the church, which is by custom reserved for those who are weaker. I thought, Since you are going to die, you should still try to last another two or three days. That is why we parted.

But there is another reason, a little delicate to explain, for why we separated, and that I ought to add. Here it is. When everyone in a family must die, when you can do nothing to save your wife or ease her agony, and it's the same for her, it's better to go get yourself killed somewhere else. I will say what I mean more precisely. If you will not be dying first, if you will hear the cries of your papa, your mama, the screams of your wife or child, and if you cannot lift a hand to save them, or even to help them die easier, you in turn will die in the wreckage of the feelings you shared in the good times, because you will feel too guilty for a situation that is utterly beyond you. At the final moment, an unbearable sense of shame will possess you, overwhelming love, fidelity, and all such emotions. At the very last edge of existence, you will be robbed of even the memories of your moments of joy. That is why I thought it might be better that we should be cut, all of us, out of one another's sight.

On Kayumba Hill, things turned serious right away. It's a eucalyptus forest, as I mentioned. Eucalyptuses are tall trees that grow too widely spaced for anyone to hide among them, unlike the tough papyrus in the marshes. Well, the bottom of the hill was encircled by *interahamwe*. Every morning, they would come up in rows, singing, and they began the chase with shouts. To escape them you had to take off, do the hundred-yard dash in under nine seconds. You needed to nip in and out among the trees, dodging pursuers all day long, without ever losing speed.

Often, they set up ambushes. Some of them would take cover silently someplace, while their colleagues would rush up behind us to drive us like antelopes toward the tricksters lying in wait. And that way they could kill more of us. Sort of like Kilimanjaro safaris, without the cameras. So, you had to run without ever letting down your guard, you had to pick up a certain technique, and here it is.

As I said, the *interahamwe* were crafty. Therefore, you yourself had to organize even more clever countertactics. When we heard them climbing up, since they were yelling and singing, we'd let them get within about a few hundred yards. At that distance, an arrow isn't of major concern. Then you would pretend to run away, and circle back around them at tip-top speed. They themselves would keep hunting those who were not fleet enough and who fled straight ahead, and that way you, behind their backs, would earn a most useful rest. After two or three hours, a fresh line of attack would come up to finish off the wounded, and you would get around them again. That's how young people with nimble legs that could cleave the air tried to save themselves. As for the others, their only chance was to dash onward until they ran out of breath, hoping not to be cut down before the end.

At around four o'clock, the criminals would return to town, because they were afraid of the dark. Up on the hill, in the evening, we'd hear them enjoying themselves with songs and drinks. We could see that they now lived in the most comfortable houses. Sometimes, on the breeze, we could even smell roasting meat. As for us, we'd go forage in the fields, and we slept outdoors in the rain, under branches.

The following morning, up they would come again, singing, and the all-day chase would resume. We attempted to run in little groups to give ourselves some courage. Anyone caught in an ambush was killed; anyone who twisted an ankle was killed; anyone afflicted with fever or diarrhea was killed.

Every evening, the forest was littered with dozens of the dead and the dying.

But our fate was doubly cruel, because even though the rains had come, we found no water to drink on the hill, for lack of containers. In the beginning, we could slake our thirst thanks to sheets of corrugated metal, but later this roofing material was carried off for use in the houses in town, and we could not figure out how to collect water anymore. Except by licking wet leaves. We did not have the advantage of standing water, like our compatriots down in the marshes. So at the end of a long day's running, as soon as a survivor tried to enjoy the relief of freedom, he immediately felt parched. I might add that more and more people were dying simply of thirst, in the midst of the rainy season.

In the forest, we gathered together by acquaintance or through fate. We were filthy with mud because we could no longer clean ourselves. There were mamas who had lost their pagnes, girls who wrapped their underwear around their heads for protection against the sun. Some people suffered from festering wounds. When quiet returned in the evenings, we used to sit next to one another to hunt lice and rub dirt from our skin. We never felt humiliated by that, though. We were all enduring the same hardship, and never saw anyone clean enough to make the rest of us look dirtier. Sometimes we even found the heart for teasing. A mama would sit down beside you, to delouse you, and she'd say, "Ah, you're so grubby it's impossible to tell for sure if you're black," or some joke like that. The only thing that counted was to survive a little bit longer.

At times, on the hill, we would watch the Hutus carousing over in Nyamata, during a wedding, for example. And we would even say, right out loud, "If they let us live out our lives here, like animals, just not killing us, that would be fine. Let them take our houses, let them kill our cows, that's nothing. If they'd stop killing us, that would be fine."

People harbor mysterious reasons for wanting to survive. The more we died, the more we were prepared to die—and the faster we ran to win a moment of life. Even those who'd had their arms and legs cut off, they asked for water to last only one more hour. I cannot explain this phenomenon. It's not an animal reflex, because animals, they want to live because they aren't ever aware that they will die, since they do not know what death is. For us, if I may put it clumsily, the will to live is a fearsome primordial desire.

However, I believe that seeing us like that, living like worthless wild things, made the Hutus' work easier for them. Especially for those who were not consumed with a killing hatred.

One day a group of us surprised three Hutus. They hadn't been paying attention, had let themselves be left on their own. When we surrounded them, they sat down on some leaves. There was a guy among us who ran up carrying some arrows he'd found on the ground. "All right," we said, "your luck has turned: this time we're the ones going to kill you." An old man begged us, "No, no, please, don't kill us!" I said to him, "And just why not? You spend your days cutting us— and now you're crying so you won't be stuck full of arrows?"

He told me, "It's not my fault, it's the commune that wants this. It's down there that they make us do all this." I asked him, "If that's true, why don't you come pass the whole time until the evening in the shade—without killing, in any case—and then go back down to Nyamata all rested and so keep the approval of the authorities?" His reply to me was, "That is a good idea, I hadn't thought of that." I started to yell, I was incensed: "It never occurred to you that you could simply not kill us?" He answered, "No: from killing so much, we forgot to think about you."

I now believe that this Hutu harbored no savagery in his heart. Whereas we lay on our bellies to scrabble in the earth for manioc and were constantly bolting at the slightest sound, eaten alive by lice, dying hacked up by machetes like goats at the market. We seemed like animals because we no longer resembled the human beings we had once been, and the Hutus —they had grown used to seeing us as animals. They tracked us like that. And the truth is, they are the ones who had turned into animals. They had robbed the Tutsis of their humanity in order to kill them more comfortably, but they themselves had sunk lower than wild beasts because they no longer knew why they were killing and because in doing so, they were becoming crazed. An *interahamwe*, when he caught a pregnant Tutsi, he began by cutting into her belly. Not even the spotted hyena imagines that kind of viciousness with his fangs.

In Kayumba Forest, we lived as one community. We couldn't steal anything from one another, or squabble over nothing. People who hadn't gotten along together before because of bickering forgot their problems. I remember two bothersome disputes. One because of a huge man who growled nastily when anyone came near his food pot. The other? The fault of a young man who insulted his sister and refused to feed her because she wasn't good at scrounging for food in the fields. Two mean idiots out of thousands of people, nothing for us to fight about.

When we slept beside one another, even if we had stripped naked to wash our shorts, we felt no desire to fool around; we didn't think about sex and its fantasies because we had all seen too much blood during the day. We suffered the same fate, faced the same danger, and since we were bound to die, we tried to remain good friends for as long as we could. Sometimes, now, I tell myself that if men and women were as kind to one another on this earth as we were in Kayumba, the world would be so much more merciful than it is. But all those people who lived in peace together are dead, and they aren't even buried.

Today, in the district, we know of Hutus who were obliged to kill their Tutsi families to escape death themselves, but there is only a single case of a Tutsi who killed Tutsis in an attempt to save himself, one person out of a few tens of thousands of people. This guy was a very popular player for Bugesera Sport, the regional soccer team. He tried to become an *interahamwe* by denouncing his neighbors; he helped out with the killing, thinking to avoid that fate thanks to his former teammates. The *interahamwe* used him and, at the last minute, they cut him down, laying him out across a road.

We knew offering to join them was useless because they didn't need that, and made no exceptions. Even the girls who were kept to be raped or do housework, they were taken only by ordinary Hutus, and as soon as the *interahamwe* noticed this, they swiftly killed them without a word to their owners. In Nyamata, I know of just two girls who escaped after being kept with the families of killers. I'm not talking about any who might have been well-hidden.

The Hutus were quite determined to complete our extermination. When captured, we Tutsis never betrayed anyone, because we knew it wouldn't get us anywhere. Someone offering to reveal the hiding place of an acquaintance might well be cut most cruelly, as a thank-you, to make the killers laugh. So we often died without a fight, without even speaking, save for the inevitable cries of pain. As if we had gotten used to death before being struck down.

One day, I remember, I was concealed behind a tumbledown house. Some *interahamwe* went inside and found a family there. I heard blades hitting bone, but I could barely hear the moans. Then they discovered a child behind a well. It was a little girl. They began to cut her. I could listen to everything in my hiding-place. She didn't even beg for mercy to try to save herself, simply murmured little words before she died— "Jesus," I think, or something like that, then simple faint cries.

So, why did they hack people into pieces instead of killing them straight off? I don't think it was to punish them for trying to escape. Or to discourage the living from running, from dodging the slaughterers all day long, from saving themselves in any way they could. Or maybe they did so for only a tiny percentage of their victims. That trash thought they would be finishing us all off in any case.

They cut us out of a taste for barbarity, nothing more. Among them there were ordinary Hutus who killed in an ordinary way, malicious Hutus who killed maliciously—usually *interahamwe*, and finally, extremists in cruelty who killed with extreme cruelty.

Every morning, even on Sundays, the hunters came up on various paths, wearing hats, their blades on their shoulders, singing. In the late afternoon, around four, they would go home, chatting away, leaving behind one or two hundred corpses beneath the eucalyptus trees. Old people and children at first, then the sick, those who were growing weaker, then the women, and those whose luck had run out. Several teams tried to escape by night toward Burundi; two men survived: a sturdy cattleman who killed the guy trying to kill him and wound up crossing into Burundi in his flight without knowing it, and Théoneste, who threaded his way through the bush thanks to a thousand cowherd's tricks.

In Kayumba we heard talk of suicide on certain evenings. Old folks who had lived through too many threats since 1959 and felt they'd had enough. Young people who wanted to escape the machete, preferring to die deep in the river without having to plead in torment with their killers. But such cases were much rarer than in the marshes. First, because we saw too many dead bodies during the day to want to add any more; second, because there wasn't anything handy to kill ourselves with. Just one time, on a day of sadness, I resolved to end it all and go throw myself into the Nyabarongo. On my way down, I had to make a sudden detour to avoid a team of *interahamwe* that had appeared out of nowhere. In a sense, I owe them my life.

Suicide in Kayumba required great courage, energy, and luck. But there were mamas and papas who, one day, would refuse to run. I was behind a rock one morning with a mama who was still young and strong. When we heard the hue and cry of the murderers, I stood up; she sat still. I told her, "Hurry, we'll get caught." She answered softly, "Go on, Innocent. Me, this time I'm not moving anymore." I ran. When I returned to the rock that evening, her head had been chopped off.

In the end, only we sprinters were left. We had begun with five or six thousand; one month later, when the *inkotanyi* arrived, there were twenty of us. That's the arithmetic. If the *inkotanyi* had dawdled another week along the way, there would have been exactly zero still alive. And the whole Bugesera would be a desert, because the Hutus had grown so used to killing that they would have gone on to murder one another.

Personally, I would just like to point out to those who split hairs about the Rwandan genocide that if the Hutus had not been so preoccupied with lining their pockets, they would have succeeded in exterminating all the Tutsis in the country. It was our good luck that they wasted lots of time removing sheets of metal roofing, looting houses, and arguing over the spoils. What's more, when a group of *interahamwe* had struck it rich, they threw a party: they feasted to cheer themselves up, they drank, they smoked to ease digestion, and took the next day off.

Many foreign journalists have said that beer and suchlike played a decisive role in the killings. That's right, but in a way completely backward from what they imagined. To a certain extent, many of us owe our survival to the Primus, to which we can offer our thanks.

Let me explain. The killers would turn up sober in the morning to begin killing. In the evening, however, they downed more Primus than usual, to reward themselves, and that slowed them up the next day. The more they killed, the more they stole, the more they drank. Perhaps to relax, perhaps to forget or to congratulate themselves. Be that as it may, the more they cut, the more they drank in the evening, the farther behind they fell in their schedule. No doubt about it: that foolishness with looting and drunkenness is what saved our lives.

As for us, the survivors of Kayumba, we pursue different activities today. Time moves us apart, but we continue to visit and encourage one another, we speak of the bravery we displayed up there. Those who frequent *cabarets* share a Primus and discuss all that. We still cannot fathom what happened to us.

I see that in Africa, the more ethnic groups there are, the more people talk about them and the fewer problems they pose. Throughout the world, if you are white, or black, from the North Pole or the jungle, you inspire no contagious anxiety. Here in Rwanda, it's a big deal to be Hutu or Tutsi. In a marketplace, a Hutu can spot a Tutsi at fifty yards, and vice versa, but admitting that there is a difference is taboo, even among ourselves. The genocide will change the lives of several generations of Rwandans, yet it is still not mentioned in our schoolbooks. We ourselves are never at ease with these differences, and in a manner of speaking, ethnicity is like AIDS: the less you talk about it, the more havoc it wreaks.

I have read that after every genocide, the historians explain that it will be the last. Because no one will ever be able to accept such an outrage again. Well, that is a big fat joke. Those responsible for the genocide in Rwanda are neither poor and ignorant farmers, nor ferocious and drunken *interahamwe*. The culprits are educated people. The teachers, the politicians, the journalists who went abroad to Europe to study the French Revolution and the humanities. Those who have traveled, who are invited to conferences and who have invited White guests to dinner in their gracious homes. The intellectuals who bought floor-to-ceiling bookcases. They themselves rarely killed with their own hands, but they sent others out to the hills to do the work.

In Nyamata, the Christian name of the president of the *interahamwe* was Joseph-Désiré. He was a good teacher. We used to share a Primus now and then, in friendship. He would tell us, "Well, if the *inkotanyi* come into Rwanda, we will be forced to kill you," and suchlike things. But since he was nice, we'd laugh about it and offer him another beer. This man, with whom we'd tell funny stories, later proved to be one of the three or four major promoters of the genocide in the region.

Genocide is not really a matter of poverty or lack of education, and I will tell you why. I am a teacher, so I think that education is necessary to enlighten us about the world. But education does not make someone better; it makes that person more efficient. Anyone who wishes to foment evil will find an advantage in knowing about man's obsessions, learning about his nature, studying sociology. The educated man—if his heart is flawed, if he seethes with hatred—will do more harm. In 1959, Hutus had relentlessly robbed, killed, and driven away Tutsis, but they had never for a single day imagined exterminating them. The intellectuals are the ones who emancipated the Hutus, if I may put it that way, by planting the idea of genocide in their heads and sweeping away their hesitations. I do not deny the injustices suffered by Hutus during the reign of the Tutsi kings, or the excesses of wealth and authority during that time. But that time is so bygone that not a single Rwandan historian capable of writing a decent book on those royal days has ever earned a diploma from the national university in Butare.

Anyway, the Tutsis have not committed any malicious actions since 1959, because after the elections, the soldiers became Hutus, and so did the mayors, the police chiefs and officers, and even the local postmasters. The Tutsis, they enlarged their herds, taught in their classrooms, developed their businesses, and got used to letting themselves be humiliated on ceremonial occasions. So it is Hutu intellectuals without any grievances who planned the eradication of the Tutsis.

Besides, since the French were advising our army, some of them knew that the genocide was in the works. Supposedly, they didn't believe in it, yet many Whites were familiar with the plan and with Habyarimana's character, just as they knew about Hitler's. One day, in Nyamata, white armored cars arrived to collect the White priests. Out in the main street, the *interahamwe* thought these vehicles had come to punish them, and they fled, yelling to one another that the Whites were going to kill them. The armored cars never even stopped for a quick Primus to have a laugh over the misunderstanding. And a few weeks later, the Whites sent professional photographers to show the world how we'd been massacred. So, you can understand that a feeling of abandonment has found its way into the hearts of our survivors, and that it will never go away. But I don't want to irritate you with all that.

Me, I see today that there is still uneasiness in talking about the survivors, even among Rwandans, even among Tutsis. I think that everyone would like the survivors to relinquish the genocide, in a way. As if people wanted them to leave the task of dealing with it to others, who have never been in direct danger of being sliced up by machete. As if we were from now on somewhat superfluous. But it must be said that we are also at fault in this matter. After the genocide, we were profoundly apathetic, and we lost out.

There was a boy in the forest who had managed to save a radio and some batteries. During the first week, in the evenings, we would sometimes hear news about the genocide. We listened to a speech by the interim prime minister in which he scolded the Hutus of Butare because they had to be coaxed into killing. Later, there was a speech by the minister of agriculture, who advised farmers always to work with a blade within reach, in case a Tutsi fugitive passed through their fields. We heard of the disasters in the North, in the South. We thought, up among our eucalyptus trees, that we were among the last survivors.

So, when we came down, we told ourselves, We were supposed to die, we are still here, that's enough for us: Why work, or fend for ourselves, or speak out? Me, I was done in by all that running on Kayumba, weakened by malaria, despondent over the death of my family. As if those misfortunes were not enough, my leg was blown off in a street by a mine. I no longer sought chances to spend time with people from the outside, cameramen and the like. I didn't give a hang for them, for me, for us survivors, for whatever might have been worth saying among ourselves.

In addition, some of us had reeking wounds that were disgusting to approach, while others found themselves beggars, and others could no longer offer hospitality, having no roof over their heads. We preferred to stay home with our own kind. As soon as we scraped a few coins together, we downed some Primus. Reporters went by our doors without even knocking, because they were too busy to bother with people who never talked anymore. The Tutsis repatriated from Burundi were in better shape than we were—they had managed to cling to more normal lives, and showed more obliging faces, so people took greater notice of them.

One thing that surprises me now is that many who promoted the genocide have turned back into everyday people, quietly spreading themselves around, sauntering down streets, in Kenya, in Europe, in France. They teach in universities, they preach in churches or doctor patients in hospitals, and in the evening, they listen to music, they supervise children's homework. People say, "The genocide, it's sheer human madness," but the police don't even go question the star performers of the genocide in their villas in Brussels or Nairobi. If you notice one of them in Paris, in a fashionable suit and wearing gold-rimmed glasses, you think, Well, now there's a sophisticated African gentleman. You do not say to yourself, There is a sadist who stockpiled two thousand machetes, then handed them out to the peasants of his native hill. And so, because of this neglected duty, the killings can begin again, here or elsewhere.

War is a matter of intelligence and stupidity. Genocide is a matter of the breakdown of intelligence. One thing that always baffles me, whenever I talk about those times, is the viciousness of the slaughter. If there was killing to be done, they had only to kill, but why cut off arms and legs?

Those who did that were not demons, or drug-crazed *interahamwe*, as the Whites kept saying. They were neighbors with whom we used to chat while walking to the market. In one place, they ran five or six Tutsis through with a long sharp pole to make them die like skewered meat. Now, apparently, in the prison in Rilima, they claim not to remember how they could have done those incredible things. But they remember everything, down to the last detail.

I feel, I repeat, that they cut and mutilated to take humanity away from the Tutsis and kill them more easily that way. And they made a dreadful mistake. I learned for example of a killer who had buried his Tutsi neighbor completely alive in a hole behind the man's house. Eight months later, he felt himself called by his victim in a dream. He went back to that garden, he dug up the dirt, unearthed the corpse, and got himself arrested. Since then, in the prison, he wanders day and night with that man's skull in a plastic bag he holds tight in his hand. He cannot let go of the bag even to eat. He is haunted to the last extremity. When you have burned little children alive in front of the church in Nyamata, and organized hunts to kill oldsters in the forest, and sliced babies out of pregnant girls in the marshes, you cannot claim to have forgotten how you could have done that, or that you were made to do it.

I think, moreover, that Rwanda eats meagerly twice a day thanks only to its agriculture; that it takes many arms and strong hands to keep the bush from getting the upper hand; and that this truth about the soil must temper the need for justice.

I also see that a gulf is opening between those who lived through the genocide and everyone else. Someone from outside, even a Rwandan, even a Tutsi, whose whole family was lost in the slaughter, this person cannot completely understand the genocide. Even someone who has seen all those bodies rotting in the bush, after the liberation, and the heaped-up corpses in the churches—this person cannot look at life with our eyes.

Foreigners as well as Rwandans who have returned home say that the survivors are growing bitter, withdrawn, almost aggressive. But this is not true: we are simply rather disheartened because we gradually let ourselves become isolated. We survivors, we are growing more like strangers in our own land—which we have never left—than all the foreigners and expatriates who consider us so anxiously.

A Rwandan outside of the genocide, he thinks that everything the survivor says is true, but even so, a bit exaggerated. He believes whatever the survivor tells him and then, a moment later, he begins to forget. He accepts the principle of the genocide, but has doubts about the details. Anyone who has not experienced the genocide wants life to go on as before, wants to press on toward the future without too many delays. To a passing stranger, he gives advice: "Well, it's good to listen to the survivors, but to best understand the situation, you must hear what the others have to say." The Tutsi from away, who lived in Bujumbura during the genocide, or in Kampala, or Brussels, does not understand these commemorations, these ceremonies of mourning, these memorials. He tires of these constant observances, he does not want his conscience to traumatize him relentlessly. He does not want to see life darkly, and that's understandable. To a survivor, he recommends, "My friend, stop brooding, try to forget, think of yourself now." Some of them can even say, "At least do it for those who were killed," or similar suggestions, to ease forgetting. But the survivor does not want to forget.

In time, a survivor's memory changes, but not in the same way for everyone. Certain details are forgotten, others get mixed together. Dates and places become confused. A person will tell you one time about being struck over and over with a machete, and the next time about a single blow from a club. It's just a different way of remembering, of telling what happened. People forget things, but then again, they learn new information by hearsay.

On the one hand, people are no longer interested in talking about certain events, while on the other, they gradually find the courage to speak of things they had kept hidden, such as being raped, or abandoning a baby as they ran away. The faces of friends or relatives may fade, but that doesn't mean we are starting to neglect them. For we forget nothing. Me, I may spend a few weeks without seeing again the faces of my dead wife and children, whereas before I had dreamed of them every night. But not for a single day do I forget that they are no longer here, that they were cut, that those others tried to wipe us out, that in the space of a few hours, our longtime neighbors turned into animals. Every single day, I say the word: genocide.

A survivor cannot help always thinking back to the genocide. For someone who did not experience it, there is before, during, and after the genocide, and it's all a life being lived in different ways. For us, there is before, during, and after, but they are three different lives, and they have broken apart forever. Even if one of us shows joy in resuming previous activities and joins hands with a man or woman from the neighborhood to move ahead faster, the survivor knows, deep inside, that this performance is a fraud. It is the same, and even more, for a person who speaks only of forgiving, forgetting, and the like.

I believe that in the survivor, during the genocide, something mysterious in the heart's core has become blocked. Survivors know that they will never learn what this is. So they want to talk about it constantly. There is always something new to say and hear. Someone who was in Kibuye, for example, and who tells how it was in Kibuye, is answered by someone else telling how it was in Cyangugu, and this can never end.

The survivors tend not to believe that they are truly alive anymore—in other words, that they're still the same people they were before, and in a way, that's a little how they keep going.

A SHOP ON MAIN STREET

In Nyamata, the friendliest *cabaret* is not a *cabaret*: it's Marie-Louise's shop. Prudence (the name written on the front wall of the establishment) sits across from the marketplace and next to a real *cabaret*, La Fraternité, which—in spite of the pleasant atmosphere of its bowered patio, its exotic frescoes, its starry sky—is as deserted as the other cafés in town. Marie-Louise's cramped little shop, on the other hand, its faded green walls lighted in the evening by a single neon bulb, is always packed with customers.

At the back of the room hang lengths of magnificent Rwandan cloth in a palette of blues, as well as some gaily colored Congolese fabrics. Piled upon the shelves are thermoses, purses, underwear, bags of rice, notebooks, padlocks. . . . A tall glass case displays ballpoint pens, batteries, shampoos. A refrigerator hums against a wall. In the slow hours of the afternoon, the proprietress may be found sitting outside on a bench, gazing idly at the square; in the evening, behind her counter, she favors a comfortable armchair. Marie-Louise has a kind face. She dresses with traditional Rwandan elegance, and speaks in a sweet, languid voice.

Just inside the shop door are a couch, a bench, and some stools clustered around a low table. From the noon break until late into the night, people stop by for a drink. A group of local intellectuals meets here, as well as the veterans of Kayumba, plus shopkeepers and regular customers from the main street. Most faithful of all are those stalwarts who would never let a day go by without dropping in: Innocent, of course; Sylvère and Gonzalve, two school principals; Benoît, a stockbreeder, in boots and cowboy hat; André, the deputy public prosecutor, a discreet man with a dry, sarcastic wit; Tite, former star of the big soccer team that made it to the first division, now a coach; not forgetting Jean, a tireless chauffeur and Marie-Louise's good right arm; and the priceless Englebert who, if he did not exist, would simply have to be invented. A young man from a prominent family (of royal blood, he sometimes announces over his third beer), a polyglot and erudite high-ranking civil servant when sober, Englebert fled the massacres in the capital and hid in the marshes of Nyamata. Since then, nothing and no one can persuade him to return to the city and his office. He spends half his time living like a hermit in a hovel lost in the woods. When he's not helping edit little projects in return for a Primus, he divides the rest of his time between Marie-Louise's shop (on lucky days) and the *urwagwa* dives, desperately seeking an ever-receding past, quoting Shakespeare and Baudelaire, playing—and rather drolly—the role of class clown or village idiot.

Marie-Louise knows everyone's "usual": lukewarm Primus for Innocent, chilled Amstel for Sylvère, a tall Mutzig for

Dominique, a short one for Benoît. . . . She brings fresh bottles while simultaneously waiting on the housewives at her counter and coddling a child with no pocket money. Sipping her Coca-Cola, she joins in the discussions: in her shop, people review the latest local gossip and radio newscasts, and there is lots of joking around. As beer follows beer, customers begin telling stories about the genocide, recalling memories of memories, laughing about some triumph or disaster. This complicity, the often edgy humor, and the impressive mutual tolerance everyone observes create an atmosphere the regulars have come to depend on. Marie-Louise's shop is also a place where people can leave messages, and share a glass in mourning or to celebrate a baptism.

Why at Marie-Louise's and not at La Fraternité? Or in the always deserted but lovely garden of L'Intzinsi, or the Podium, all formerly so popular? The first reason springs from an early reaction right after the genocide, when the town seemed like something devastated by a hurricane. Survivors were coping with destitution, while those returning from exile in Burundi, unable to get their bearings, were wary of this depopulated and traumatized place. As for the Hutus coming home from Congo, they no longer dared come into town for fear of reprisals or denunciations, and kept to themselves up on their hills. The *cabarets* remained silent, the empty terraces proclaiming all too clearly the absence of the missing and the imprisoned. Nyamata's drinkers preferred instinctively to gather in stores, beverage warehouses, workshops, in more intimate, less haunted spaces, where beer costs a little less, too. Many thus found themselves at the shop run by Marie-Louise, whose late husband had been the most prosperous shipper in the region.

That first impulse became a habit. L'Intzinsi and the bar in the cultural center, once favored by extremists, have been dropped, despite new owners. The Podium has not reopened. Neither Le Club nor La Fraternité can "ambience" anymore. Only the dreary bistros on little side streets, offering tart banana beer at quite modest prices, have won back a faithful clientele.

The second reason for the success of Marie-Louise's shop is of course the tact and kindness of the "boss-lady": her perpetual smile, her affection for her guests, and her discretion when she wipes the slate clean for the most down-and-out of her customers, sends a drowsy drinker home, or nips an argument in the bud with a witty remark. As Innocent deftly puts it, not enough superlatives survived the genocide to describe the good nature of Marie-Louise, whom no one would now dare betray for a different *cabaret*.

MARIE-LOUISE KAGOYIRE,

45 Years Old, Shopkeeper
The Main Street of Nyamata

My parents were small farmers and livestock breeders. They gave me permission to finish my first year in secondary school before starting to look for a husband. In our customs, girls marry earlier when the parents aren't rich.

One day, I came to visit a maternal aunt in Nyamata. On the main square, a gentleman noticed me and liked what he saw. His name was Léonard Rwerekana, and he was already a successful businessman. We began winking at each other, on a few occasions. Still, in those days, the girl was not supposed to accept any kind of advances directly, so he asked my aunt to be the go-between and she pressed his case with my family. The gentleman walked an entire day in the sun to go visit my parents—who said that a man who had come on foot should not be made to cool his heels any longer. I got married when I was nineteen years old.

At the time, Nyamata was a straggling village of mud-brick houses with sheet-metal roofs. It wasn't until 1974 that buildings of stone and concrete appeared. Léonard constructed his

first house on our lot, then a warehouse on the main street, followed by some new stores. In 1976 he bought a van, an old, used van, but it was the first private vehicle. Then he opened the *cabaret* La Fraternité and some restaurants, developed the trade in beans and beverages, bought some fields and cattle. In 1980, with two new vans out on the road, he was the most important shipper in the area. Mounting jealousy was already coming between the Tutsi and Hutu business communities, because the Tutsis were prospering faster than the Hutus. One reason for this was that the Hutus coming from Gitarama didn't know any of the customers in Nyamata. Another reason was that the Tutsis kept their clerks on for five or six years, until they were able to open their own little businesses, whereas the Hutus were always turning over their employees. But the most important thing was that the Tutsis worked with their inventory on hand and never borrowed money from anyone.

The day of the plane crash, it became difficult for Tutsis who lived in the center of town to leave. Lots of people sought protection within the solid wall around our house. Léonard had lived through several massacres in his youth, so he knew that this time the situation was out of control, and he advised the young people to sneak off up to Kayumba. But he himself no longer wanted to flee, and said that his legs had already run enough as it was.

On the morning of April 11, the first day of the massacres, the *interahamwe* showed up making a big commotion right outside our front gate. Léonard took the keys to go open it without making them wait, thinking to thus save the women and children. A soldier shot him down before he said a first word. The *interahamwe* poured into our courtyard, caught all the children they could, lined them up, laid them out on the ground, and began to butcher them. They even killed a Hutu boy, the son of a colonel, who had been playing there with some pals. I myself had managed to get around to the back of the house with my mother-in-law, and we lay down behind piles of tires. The killers didn't finish the job, because they were in too much of a hurry to start looting. We could hear them getting into the cars, the vans, loading cases of Primus, fighting over the furniture and everything else, rummaging under the beds for money.

That evening, my mother-in-law left her hiding-place and sat down in front of the tires. Some young men saw her there and asked, "Mama, what are you doing here?" She replied, "I'm not doing anything anymore, since from now on I am alone." They took her, they cut her, they carried away all that was left in the bedrooms and the parlor. They set a fire, and that's why they forgot about me.

In the courtyard was a child who had not been killed. I leaned a ladder against the wall our house shared with the enclosure next door and I climbed up with the child to jump down into my neighbor Florient's courtyard, which was empty. I hid the child in the woodshed and huddled inside the doghouse. On the third morning I heard footsteps, and recognizing my neighbor, I came out. "Marie-Louise," he exclaimed, "they're killing everyone in the town, your house has burned up, and you—you're here? But now what is there I can do for you?" I said, "Florient, do this for me: kill me. But don't

126

reveal me to the *interahamwe* who will strip me and cut me to pieces."

This Monsieur Florient was a Hutu. He was the military intelligence chief of the Bugesera, but he had built his house on our land, and before the war we had spoken kindly with one another, we had shared some good times, and our children had mingled freely in our two yards. So, he shut the child and me inside his house, gave us something to eat, and left. The next day he warned me: "Marie-Louise, they're checking the corpses in town, they cannot find your face, and they're looking for you. You must leave here, because if they catch you in my home, they will rob me in turn of my life."

He took us at night to a Hutu woman he knew, who was hiding a small group of her Tutsi acquaintances. One day, the *interahamwe* came knocking on her door to search the house. The lady went to talk to them, came back, and asked, "Does anyone here have any money?" I gave her a wad of bills I had tucked into my pagne. After taking a small sum for herself, she returned to the *interahamwe*, who went away. Every day, the negotiation would begin again, and the lady was growing very nervous. Then one day Monsieur Florient brought another warning: "Marie-Louise, the young people in town, they want you too much, you must leave." I said again to him, "Florient, you have the means, kill me, I want to die in a house. Do not let me fall into the hands of the *interahamwe*." He said, "I will not kill my wife's friend. If I find a vehicle, will you have money for payment?" I gave him another roll of bills I had, which he counted, saying, "This, this is something, they should accept it." He came back and made an offer: "You'll be put into a sack and taken into the forest. Then you'll be on your own." Then right away he said, "The *interahamwe* pillaged your house, the soldiers will go off with the money, and I who am saving you, I will come out of it with nothing: Is that really proper?" So then I told him, "Florient, I have two villas in Kigali: take them. The big store on the street, I leave it to you. I will sign papers procuring all this for you. But I want you to go with me toward Burundi."

We left, with me lying down in the military van between the driver and Florient. First I stayed in his house at the military camp in Gako. I was locked in a room. While everyone was sleeping, someone would bring me food. I had only one pagne to wear. That lasted for weeks, I no longer remember how long. One night, a friend of Florient's arrived with news. "The *inkotanyi* are coming in fast, we'll be evacuating the barracks. Keeping you has become too prickly, I have to take you away." He had me climb into a truck that was delivering sacks to the front. We drove off—all roadblocks opened at our passage—and into a dark forest, where the driver stopped beneath the trees. I was shaking and told him, "Well, I have nothing left. It's my turn to die. At least if it's quick, all right." He replied, "Marie-Louise, I'm not going to kill you, because I work for Florient. Make your way straight ahead, don't ever stop. At the end of the forest, you will place your hand on the barrier at our border with Burundi, and deliverance." I trudged along, I fell, I crawled on my hands and knees. When I reached the border crossing, I heard voices calling in the darkness, and I fell asleep.

Later, a Burundian associate of my husband's came to get me in a van at a refugee camp. When he saw me, he did not recognize me. He did not even want to believe that I was Léonard's wife. I had lost forty-four pounds, I was wearing a pagne made from sacking, I had swollen feet and hair crawling with lice.

Monsieur Florient is now awaiting trial in the penitentiary at Rilima. He was an officer. He left every morning and returned at night with stories of how the killings were going in the town. I saw, in the corridor, piles of new axes and machetes. He spent my money, he looted my merchandise. In spite of that, never will I go to accuse him of anything in a courtroom, because when everyone thought only of killing, he saved one life.

I came back to Nyamata at the end of the genocide, in July. No one left in my family in Mugesera, no family alive in Nyamata, the neighbors killed, the warehouse pillaged, the trucks stolen. I had lost everything; life meant nothing to me. Nyamata was desolate, because all the roofs, all the doors and windows had been removed. But above all it was time itself that seemed broken in the town, as if time had stopped forever— or on the contrary had slipped away much too quickly while we were gone. I mean that we no longer knew when the whole business had begun, how many days and nights it had all lasted, what season we were in, and to tell the truth we just didn't care. The children would go off into the thickets to catch chickens; we began to eat a little meat, we set to making repairs, tried to settle back into at least a few old habits. From then on we concentrated on the day at hand, caught up in searching for groups of friends with whom we could spend the night, so we wouldn't die all alone in a nightmare.

One morning, some friends brought me money and said, "Marie-Louise, take this. You're good at bargaining, and we aren't. You must take up business again." I had a door put on this little shop; the trade came back, but the hope was gone. In the old days, prosperity held out its arms to me. Léonard and I, we went from one project to the next, our plans did well, we were loved and respected. Now I see all life with a somber eye, watching out everywhere for dangers large and small. I have lost the one who loved me, and can find no one left to help me bear up.

In the shop, customers tell me how they survived. In the evening, I hear acquaintances discussing the massacres. And I still don't understand a thing about any of it. With the Hutus, we shared and shared alike, attended christenings and marriages—and then suddenly they went on a rampage like wild beasts. I don't believe in the jealousy explanation, because envy has never driven anyone to lay children in a row in a courtyard and crush them with clubs. I don't believe in that talk about beauty and a feeling of inferiority. In the hills, Tutsi and Hutu women alike were muddied and worn out by the fields; in the town, Tutsi and Hutu children were equally smiling and lovely to see.

The Hutus had the good fortune to monopolize all the choice state jobs and favors, they reaped fine harvests because they were excellent farmers, and they opened profitable businesses, at least selling retail. We shook hands cordially over deals we struck, we lent them money, and then, they decided to hack us to pieces.

They wanted to wipe us out so much that they became obsessed with burning our photo albums during the looting, so that the dead would no longer even have a chance to have existed. To be safer, they tried to kill people and their memories, and in any case to kill the memories when they couldn't catch the people. They worked for our extermination and to erase all signs of that work, so to speak. Today, many survivors no longer possess one single little photo of their mama, their children, their baptism or marriage, a picture that could have helped them smooth a little sweetness over the pain of their loss.

Me, I see that the hatred in genocide springs solely from belonging to an ethnic group. Not from anything else, such as feelings of fear or frustration or the like. But the source of this hatred is still quite beyond to me. The *why* of hatred and genocide must not be asked of the survivors, it's too hard for them to answer. It's even too delicate a matter, they must be left to talk it over among themselves. The Hutus are the ones to ask.

Sometimes, Hutu women come back to see me, looking for work in the fields. I talk with them, I try to ask them why they wanted to kill us without ever complaining at all beforehand. But they're not having any of it. They keep saying they didn't do anything, they didn't see a thing, their men weren't *interahamwe*, and the authorities are to blame for what happened. They say our neighbors were forced to cut by the *interahamwe*, or else they would have been killed instead, and they leave it at that. I tell myself, These Hutus have killed without wavering and now they are trying to get out of discussing the truth, that's not right. Reason why I'm not sure that it can't happen all over again one day.

Everyone came out of the genocide at great cost: the Tutsis, the Hutus, the survivors, the *interahamwe*, the tradespeople, the farmers, the families, the children, all Rwandans. Maybe even the foreigners and the Whites who refused to see what was happening and took pity after the fact.

I think, moreover, that foreigners usually show pity that is all too much the same for different people who have not suffered the same misfortunes, as if the pity were more important than the misfortune. I also believe that if foreigners looked too closely at what we suffered during the genocide, they would not be able to handle their pity. Perhaps that's why they look from so far away. But that seems like the past.

It's more important that life has been shattered here, that wealth is spoiled, that no one pays attention to neighbors anymore, that people turn sad or nasty over trifles, that no one takes kindness seriously in the old way, that men are overwhelmed and women discouraged. And this is most disturbing.

Among ourselves, we never tire of talking about this post-genocide situation. We tell one another about certain moments, exchange explanations, tease one another, and if someone grows angry, we poke gentle fun to bring this person back to us. But showing our hearts to a stranger, talking about how we feel, laying bare our feelings as survivors, that shocks us beyond measure. When the exchange of words becomes too blunt, as in this moment with you, one must come to a full stop.

THE PENITENTIARY AT RILIMA

A thin cord stretched between two acacias, watched over by a guard straddling a chair, marks the entrance to the penitentiary at Rilima. Do not be fooled by this nonchalance, for no would-be escapee has ever gone beyond the neighboring forest, or nearby Lake Kidogo.

Formerly a district prison, the penitentiary today houses more than eight thousand inmates, accused or convicted of participation in the genocide in the Bugesera region, chiefly in the district of Nyamata. Living quarters for the guards and the administration are lined up in the shade. A constant back-and-forth of detainees in pink uniforms fetches cans of water on a path leading down to the lake; by the shore, inmates with privileges bathe or do laundry.

Without barbed wire or watchtowers, the outside wall of the prison sits atop a small hill. A half-open orange iron gate lets authorized prisoners slip in and out. From fifty yards away, one is struck both by the orchestral din of competing rhythms and songs and by a suffocating stench of sweat, backed up by the reek of cooking and garbage. One look through the opening in the gate gives an idea of the indescribable promiscuity of life within those walls.

Three buildings house the male prisoners; a fourth is for the female inmates. Since the population of Rilima has increased tenfold with this new influx of detainees, however, the prisoners find shelter wherever they can. Some are packed into huts and cells; most have settled into the courtyard, crowded shoulder to shoulder, some out in the sun, others under sheets of corrugated metal or plastic. It's amid this mob that the prisoners, all in pink uniforms, prepare their meals in huge cauldrons, hang out laundry, beat drums, and organize prayer meetings sponsored by priests or political meetings under the auspices of former leaders and political big shots. In this jostling throng, men compete stubbornly for space in which to weave, shape metal, play cards or checkers, gamble, pick the occasional fight, sleep, or be bored to death. Some faces are solemn, sad, perhaps despairing or full of hatred; others are resigned, cordial, even jovial.

Although they are all trapped in this overcrowding, which is often aggravated by downpours and oppressive heat, the prisoners are variously subject to different disciplinary regimes. Those who have already confessed—more than two thousand—as well as those accused of minor offenses are housed in a separate building and may circulate more freely. They tend gardens near the administration offices, repair cars, play soccer on an outdoor field, talk out under the trees. Most of those awaiting trial languish in the crowded courtyard. Others leave at dawn in a truck to work in the penitentiary's one hundred and eighty acres of fields. The men sentenced to death or to long prison terms, however, wait behind bars, and they describe this confinement, as one of them put it, as "Hell on earth."

Like all prisons housing the killers of the genocide, the one at Rilima is subject to two authorities: that of the guards, who patrol not the inner courtyard but the outside of the penitentiary, and that of the local mafia, run by former *inter-ahamwe* leaders or unrepentant ideologues of the genocide, who have re-created within Rilima the hierarchy of the Hutu militias and extremist political parties. They are the ones who manage the buildings, organize fitness exercises and festivi-ties, supervise donations, settle disputes, and offer legal ad-vice to those awaiting trial.

Without prior permission from the court or prison ad-ministration, relatives have the right to visit the prisoners—for two or three minutes: they enter in surges of two to three hundred, set down the food or clothing they've brought, ex-change a few words, and leave. The International Red Cross may inspect the entire area of the penitentiary; in return it provides, for a limited period, most of the supplies (jerry cans, basins, mattresses), medicines, and food, without which Rilima would become a "Hell on earth" for all its prisoners.

Strangely enough, the Hutus—be they villagers or towns-people, whether they admit or deny committing crimes, feel guilty or innocent—would almost seem to speak more freely about the killings while in prison than at home, doubtless because they no longer feel safe on the hills, where they might be denounced or face arbitrary arrest. In the district of Nyamata, two out of three Hutu inhabitants have come home to their lands. The others, chiefly men, were killed during the war, or haven't returned from Congo, or preferred to go back to their native villages, far from the watching eyes of their surviving neighbors. Unless those missing are in prison in Rilima.

Aside from the schools, where the children share the benches, and the marketplace, which is a necessity, and the church on Sunday, or a wake before a funeral, Hutus and Tutsis now avoid one another. On the hills, Hutu families welcome strangers with hospitality that is quite courteous, but timid and uneasy. And any reference to the genocide will drop a veil of silence over their memories, even when these families have been cleared of all suspicion by the testimony of their Tutsi neighbors.

One day, on the hill of Maranyundo, on a slope populated by Hutu families, a young woman encountered by chance becomes the exception to that code of silence. From the first moment she proves confident and talkative. She agrees to speak of her family, her Hutu village, her youth, her life as a farmer. Then, surprisingly, she does not wince and try to change the subject when the genocide is mentioned. On the contrary, without hesitation she recalls events with the perspective of an onlooker still shocked by what she has seen, describing the reactions of her neighbors, her terror of the *interahamwe*, and then her hasty flight, the mass exodus of the Hutu throngs on that long journey across a country at war to the camps in Congo, and finally her return, and her future.

Her name is Christine Nyiransabimana. With her mother and two brothers, she farms the family land. She is the unmarried mother of a boy, unwanted but cherished, as she herself explains, and of two very much wanted twin girls. Her constant smile is open and most appealing. She seems perceptive about her people. During the first visit, she alludes only in passing to the murder of her father, without any explanation. Only on the second visit does she reveal, with enigmatic reticence, why her father was killed.

CHRISTINE NYIRANSABIMANA,

22 Years Old, Farmer
Maranyundo Hill

I arrived in the area in 1980, among waves of fellow Hutus, because my parents were growing thin in Kibuye on land that was too dry and crumbly. Many Tutsis had already taken up much of the Bugesera, but new lots were still being distributed to Hutus.

When the war broke out, I was in fifth grade. At that time we'd been noticing more and more young men with grim faces who were not all local youths. They would walk into Hutu homes without giving their names and eat their fill from our cooking pots. When these *interahamwe* attacked the church in Nyamata, people gathered around to watch the slaughter. This small crowd listened to the sound of blows, the shouts of encouragement, heard the fear of those going to be cut, saw youngsters rushing to loot the priests' rooms or steal the possessions of the dead.

The spectators watched Caterpillars dump those wretched people in a big ditch, like garbage. There were voices, among the crowd, saying that certain bodies had not yet drawn their last breath, but the criminals seemed determined to finish the burial that afternoon. In the evening, they went off to eat, but the church remained surrounded by watchful lookouts. The people inside waited all night long; those with mortal wounds were waiting for death.

The *interahamwe* returned at around nine o'clock in the morning to go back to striking and stabbing anyone who was still alive. It was a kind of show that went on for two days. Many in the audience rejoiced to see the Tutsis die, shouting, "The Tutsis are finished! Get rid of those cockroaches for us!" I can also say that many people were outraged to see such vicious killing and burning. But it was quite dangerous to do more than murmur in protest, because the *interahamwe* killed—without fooling around—any Hutus having friendly dealings with their Tutsi neighbors. This, too, is true: in the crowd outside the church, those who were not enthusiastic were very frightened.

The second evening, on the way back from the church, some *interahamwe* came to the house and cut Papa down with a machete, in front of Mama and the neighbors. Papa's name was François Sayinzoga; he was a Tutsi.

In my area, and in Nyamata, I saw many Hutu relatives and neighbors kill Tutsis every day of the genocide, marauding behind the *interahamwe* or the soldiers. Coming home at night, those farmers traded boasts about their work in the marshes or forests. They would sit on chairs before their homes while their wives cooked meat, since they were slaughtering cows along with the Tutsis. They bought drink, because they were poaching money from the dead. And when they'd filled their bellies, they would chat about their day, meaning how many they'd killed. They had contests. Some would claim to have bagged two, others ten. Those who weren't killing pretended they had, so as not to be threatened themselves. I can say that everyone had the duty to kill. It was a very well-organized policy.

Every morning, people had to report to their group leader. The leader in Maranyundo, first-named Vincent, had himself called Goliath. He gave people their orders, itineraries, any special instructions for the day. Either they went along, or they would be killed. They could in fact pretend, dawdling far behind and returning in the evening without dirtying their machetes, but they had to show up coming in behind the others. Anyone who walked around doing nothing all day was not allowed to loot. Anyone claiming he had too many fields to sow on his land, anyone looking around for excuses, he could get shot down, just like that.

Reason why, also, the farmers didn't bury their victims. When they named the Tutsis they'd cut that day, if they were suspected of cheating, they had to lead the *interahamwe* to the bodies. I personally think that anyone who one day was forced to kill wanted his neighbor to be compelled the next day to kill as well, to be seen in the same light.

My family and I, we felt guilty for living amid this bloodlust, and we were truly terrified by Papa's death, so we continued working our fields in silence.

In the *cabarets*, men had begun talking about massacres in 1992. After the new political parties' first meetings, *interahamwe* committees sprang up in the communes, and the current was shut off between us. The President of Nyamata Commune was Joseph-Désiré. He visited all the Hutu homes, explaining the threat of the *inkotanyi* from Uganda, checking to see that the tools kept behind sacks of beans were well-sharpened. When Hutus drank together after political discussions, they would call Tutsis worms or cockroaches. Radio programs became quite threatening. In our house, Papa and my brothers had taken no part in talks that fanned misunderstandings, for they feared drawing venemous looks. We stayed away from the *interahamwe*, frequenting only our close neighbors, whom we had known forever. We drew water together, borrowed fire from one another, shared a beer sometimes, but we never chatted about politics.

In the region, we lived in order of our arrival: those who had come in a certain year took a certain hill; those who followed them went on to the next hill. This did not favor ethnic mixing. When people do not mingle, they don't learn enough of value about one another to get married. That's why our groups never took a marriage interest in each other. Papa and Mama, they had met in Kibuye, on the shore of Lake Kivu, before coming east.

This is another truth of importance: the *interahamwe* tried to kill all the Tutsis married to Hutus, and even peaceful Hutus mixed in with Tutsis. After Papa's death, some neighbors would threaten me because of my Tutsi blood. To avoid being killed, I considered myself Hutu, but I was scared. So, I ran away with a Hutu man to Kigali, leaving Mama and my brothers at home.

At the end of the rainy season, when the guns of the RPF could now be heard on the outskirts of Kigali, we felt that the war was reaching out for us. Some *interahamwe* killers came to loot the house, and carried all the furniture and utensils off in their rout. Some evil men who had been drinking beer raped me on the bed and left me with a baby inside. That was in May, I believe. There was tumult everywhere. Fugitives were racing by on all sides, shouting of death and alarm. Our thoughts grew frantic at all this headlong flight. Then I put on one pagne, and another, plus a sweater, and I dashed without thinking into the everyone-for-himself mêlée. We walked for at least six weeks, just kept walking, because of the alarming rumors.

All along the way, people told us that a mortal danger was at our heels, that we mustn't let it catch us. People who had money tucked away climbed up on vehicles; those without trudged on. We were emptying out, legs and feet swelling; the weakest collapsed by the side of the road to die while the others pressed on, driven by dreadful reports. We heard over and over that the soldiers in Uganda were going to avenge their Rwandan brothers and that misfortune had switched sides. We ate bananas and manioc stolen from fields and tried to cook soup from leaves. We slept on the ground. We were simply choking on fear and shame.

It was the same chaos everywhere. In June we camped for a long while in Gisenyi, by Lake Kivu and the Congolese border, before retreating to Congo. Many Whites along the roads had watched us go by. We were mistreated fugitives, and that was enough for them. I was sent to the camp in Mugunga, about six miles from Goma, where I stayed for two years.

In the camp, some of us collected wood, others cooked up the food, those who had salvaged some of their savings ran little businesses. As for me, I used to walk into Goma to do laundry in the houses of the Congolese, or work in their gardens and receive bananas and manioc in payment. At first the Congolese were pleasant to us, but they gradually hardened their hearts. Life became very bleak.

I gave birth alone, in a foreign tent, without an old mama to hold my hand, without any friend to fix me some gruel. I remained healthy with the baby, but I was having trouble eating. I was too depressed by everything that had happened. In the evening, by the fire, I would think with such longing of the family farm in Maranyundo. I yearned to go home, but the *interahamwe* spread threats throughout the camp. We still thought we would be attacked on all sides, because of the evil the soldiers and *interahamwe* had done.

Early one foggy November morning in 1997, the guns of the *banyamulinge*—the Congolese Tutsis—drove us from the camp, and that was one almighty stampede. I walked for days tagging along after a stream of people into the Masisi Mountains in eastern Congo. We fled ever deeper into fear, without knowing one another or where we were going. Then some *banyamulinge* surrounded us with guns drawn. A soldier convinced me that I would find calm in Rwanda, since I had not killed anyone, and that my house and fields were waiting for me in the neighborly atmosphere of the old days.

So, I walked in the other direction, with a road companion met by chance. On the way back, no one spoke to anyone; I crossed the country without a word. Then I had to answer questions at the town hall. Seeing Mama and my brothers alive gave me at last my first feeling of hope. They had returned long before me, since they hadn't even pushed on to Congo, and they led me straight home with great joy.

Death was still in possession of the abandoned fields. I was deeply ashamed to be seen as a Hutu, as if I were like those who had murdered so many. Even today, the same dream catches me in my sleep: north of Kigali, fleeing toward Congo, we are crossing a field choked with bodies; I step over them but more keep appearing in front of me, I continue stepping over bodies but it never ends, I go on walking over those bodies without ever getting out of the field. Then I wake up and talk with Mama, whispering to avoid awakening the children. We recall the hardships we experienced while we were apart, until we fall into the comfort of sleep.

At first, when I went to the market, I would meet hard stares and hear harsh words as I passed by. With time, the Tutsi women mourning their families and the Hutu women who feared the denunciation of their husbands' crimes have grown quiet, but people still disdain us deeply, and that hurts me. I even worry about that, because many Hutu women have soaked their hands in the blood of genocide. Men are more liable to kill and then reconcile than women. Men forget more quickly, they share the killings and the drinks more easily. Women do not yield in the same way, they keep more memories.

145

But I also know of good women, Hutus, who do not dare show compassion for the sufferings their neighbors have caused for fear of being accused as well. I know that life will not ever be serene, as before; still, when the food is good, when the children sleep well, when one feels at peace, one can forget the sadness, for just a moment. . . .

When authorities want to overthrow other authorities to take their own turn at the trough, that is a war. A genocide—that is an ethnic group that wants to bury another ethnic group. Genocide goes beyond war, because the intention lasts forever, even if it is not crowned with success. In Rwanda, there were only two main ethnic groups. So the Hutus thought it would be more convenient to be on their own to cultivate the fields and conduct business. They saw a more comfortable future simply among themselves. I believe that ignorance and greed are the cause of the catastrophe. It was not just Whites who preached envy and fear of the Tutsis to Hutus: President Habyarimana and his wife Agathe did, too—a couple who never tired of riches.

In Rwanda, we are all colored black in the same way, we eat the same red beans, and sorghum in the same season, and we sing the same hymns together in church. Hutus and Tutsis are not very different. And yet, a Hutu can easily recognize a Tutsi if he wants to find one. You start with the height, but you can be mistaken, because the Tutsi is no longer as tall as before. So you look at the face. The Tutsi's expression has a certain politeness, and his words are gentle. Even if he farms a worthless field, with an empty stomach and clothed in rags, the Tutsi always feels more middle-class, because he is descended from an ethnic group of stockbreeders. Tutsis often seem to bear themselves stiffly, so to speak, when they walk and even when greeting one another. A Tutsi likes to carry a staff with him.

The Hutu does not understand cows, and doesn't like putting in any effort over them. He doesn't celebrate in the same way. The Hutu likes to work, to eat well, to enjoy himself. Unless he's pushed to, the Hutu doesn't think of evil. He quickly makes himself comfortable. He's more easygoing or unpolished, in a way—jollier, more cheerful. He's more relaxed with things and worries less about troubles. He's neither mean nor resentful by nature.

The truth is that the Hutus loved their president too much. When he died, they did not take the time to sit down with a drink and talk, weep, keep a vigil and mourn together in our Rwandan way. It was a grievous lapse to run straightaway into the streets shouting threats. Too many radios were troubling people's minds, as I told you. Too many big men were stirring up small people. It had been planned a long time before. So, at the signal, farmers began killing and thieving, and they acquired a taste for those new activities.

And I repeat that they were forced to do that. If they tried to offer excuses or pretexts for doing their own work without getting involved in anything, they could well be killed in their fields by neighbors. On the hill, I do know some Hutus who have never cut, but none who did not join in the hunts, save for those who fled like the Tutsis.

I know some Hutus who admit their mistakes and accept their punishment. Some Hutus deny everything and think people will lose track of their killings. Others truly believe they did not kill, even though they were seen by others, bloody blade in hand: such people have gone mad from their own folly. Others do not properly weigh their own actions, as if they had done something foolish in secret but so what. One day, Mama went to the trial of one of Papa's murderers, a neighbor. He encountered Mama in the hallway of the courthouse, he said *bonjour* to her politely, asked about the family, the rains, our fields, said *au revoir*, and returned to prison as if he were going home. Mama stood there with her mouth hanging open before she started to cry.

From now on, it is impossible to follow the line of truth in what we have done. Me, I see that Evil fell upon us and that we held out our arms to it. Now I live by the hoe from Monday to Saturday. Sundays, I rest and yearn for the past. I see that I have not gotten married because of all that. And I regret it so much. I caught some children in passing, as I explained to you. I no longer really have any little problems with the neighbors. We sell one another things, we say *bonjour*, that's all.

I hope that time will help us wipe away the stains. If the Hutus try to tell the truth out loud, to offer mutual help, to go to the Tutsis and ask for forgiveness, we could hope to live together as we should, without being separated forever by what has happened.

A Secret Flight

Putting an end to the conversation with their sudden racket, a flock of scarlet-throated western bluebills and long-tailed souimanga sunbirds, with their dazzling green cloaks and blue bellies, comes parachuting into the banana plants. In front of Christine's house is a path that runs through a forest of red-flowering trees and across a muddy river via two worm-eaten trunks. Through the dense foliage, one can sometimes glimpse the round huts of the Twa pygmies, who are themselves almost never seen. Not far from Christine's family home is the former house of Odette Mukamusoni.

Odette and Christine, born one year apart on two adjacent hills, are both farmers and have children the same age. Ever since childhood, they have encountered each other on the paths to the school and the well, but they have never spoken together, although they would now have even more thoughts and memories to share, especially regarding their experiences escaping from the massacres.

Odette has recently left her hill to live in a shanty on the edge of Nyamata. Her family perished during the killings. The father of her oldest child is in exile in Congo. Vegetation has overgrown the ruins of her home and the bush has invaded the family fields, which might seem to explain why she has not returned to her village to pick up her life again. Innocent Rwililiza met her by chance near the church, in a group of volunteers unearthing bones from a mass grave to preserve them from the flooding rains. Odette was working off to one side; she seemed lost, and stunned by what she had lived through, and she told Innocent as much that day. At the time, he was not surprised by her isolation, far from her former home. He found temporary lodgings for her in a small mud hut.

During our first meeting, Odette told of her flight to the church when the killings began, her miraculous escape in the bedroom of a Brazilian nun, her hiding place under the mattress of a woman friend of her godmother's. She spoke in detail about the month she spent concealed under a bed every day, about her anguish at hearing killers chatting in the house, the waiting, the boredom, the loneliness, the latent depression, and her rescue. She wove together incidents that were certainly extraordinary, but plausible. And yet, something odd in her story awakened my suspicions: not the strangeness of her survival, or her present solitude (the fate of many traumatized survivors), but the chronological rigor, the accumulation of details, and in short, a most unlikely excellence of memory.

From the outset of the second meeting, Odette abandoned the initial version of her narrative. She admitted her fabrication, which she justified through her fear of being misunderstood by her neighbors. She offered spontaneously, and with seeming relief, to tell a true version, given here, a story as astonishing as the first tale. One episode of her flight, difficult to make public given the inevitable rumors and suspicions it would inspire, explains her initial lie, her anxiety, and her abandonment of the hill where she was born.

ODETTE MUKAMUSONI,
23 Years Old, Mason's Helper
Kanazi Hill

My father owned eight cows, but he pulled me out of primary school because I was his fourth daughter. So before the war, I was used here, there, and everywhere, for cleaning or work in the fields.

There had always been killings and house-burnings in the region, but each time we told ourselves that it would end no worse than usual. In 1994, the atmosphere changed. At the time of the first rains, we grew alarmed about the war, because our Hutu neighbors no longer returned our greetings when we met along the paths. They kept shouting threats at us: "Tutsis who see far must walk far, because soon all the Tutsis here will be killed!" In the evening, we talked cautiously about this at home, but my father refused to leave the hill, because he could not envision any future without his cows. Myself, I had found a quiet job in our capital, Kigali.

When the plane came down, I was a *boyeste*[11] in Nyakabanda, a good neighborhood in Kigali. Gloria, the mistress of the house, was a Tutsi. The husband, Joseph, was a very nice Hutu merchant. One day during the genocide, some *interahamwe* burst into the living room. The husband was off in Kenya on a business trip, and his brother was not able to plead successfully for the lady. The *interahamwe* killed the family right on the carpets. Me, I was lying hidden flat on my stomach in a little room. They didn't insist on looting because they had simply wanted to get rid of the lady and her children while the husband was gone, and that satisfied them.

An hour later, looters appeared and caught me in the house. They were getting ready to cut me up on the spot, but one of them, named Callixte, protected me from his colleagues. He was the leader, he carried a gun. He took me to be his wife because he did not have one anymore.

In his house, I would hear through the doors that the schedule of killings was going well in all the prefectures, and that there would not be a single Tutsi child left standing by the dry season. So then I told myself that if God had allowed me to keep my life in hiding so far, I shouldn't waste it. Reason why I never tried to run away at the risk of dying among the other Tutsis.

I lived in Callixte's home until the *inkotanyi* arrived in July. Afterward, he took me along in the panicky flight toward Congo, which you have heard much about. We lived first in Gisenyi, protected by the turquoise soldiers,[12] with some of Callixte's relatives. Then we traveled to Congo. We spent a year and a half in the camp at Mugunga. I was troubled by too many gruesome rumors, and I thought that from then on, I should expect nothing from life. We lived in a tent. I acted as wife to Callixte, who was never mean to me. The others in the camp knew I was Tutsi. They didn't dare say anything in front of Callixte, because he was an *interahamwe* of great importance, but when he went off on a round of meetings, I would suddenly hear worrisome and malicious gossip. One November day in 1996, I went over to a group of white trucks belonging to a humanitarian organization. Some Whites were saying that anyone who wanted to go back to Rwanda had only to get in, without paying. Callixte was off on a tour; I climbed into the back of the truck with many others. The vehicle drove to the border. Other white trucks were waiting for us behind the barriers, and that's how I retraced my way back to Nyamata.

I returned to our family land on Kanazi. Our house had been burned. Neighbors told me that there was not a single person left from my family. I learned from hearsay that Papa died not far from the house. Mama died from a spear thrown along an escape route to Burundi. I found two sisters dead in the fields. As for the others, I've heard no news about how they were killed.

The only thing I knew how to do was farming, but the land had become more stubborn while I was away. I felt too shaky and weak to plant beans. I was beyond discouraged. Hearing spiteful things behind my back about my journey to Congo, I had no idea where to turn to ask for a little help. That's why I moved to Nyamata, to a woman friend's place.

One day I heard that the rains were going to wash away the bones of those buried by the Caterpillars near the church. I joined a team to dig up the bones and put them safely away somewhere. I was looking for a little company, I wanted to seem presentable to other people. Some sympathetic residents brought bags of cement and we built the Memorial. Now I try to work as a bricklayer's helper wherever I can. When I earn a few coins, I buy yams and sorghum, and happiness returns for a moment. If not, I go visit a neighbor-lady friend, or I wait for a little luck to come my way.

I feel disoriented being the sole survivor in my family. I can't see in which direction to point my life anymore. I have a three-year-old boy, his name is Uwimana, and a three-month-old baby. They do not have Christian names[13] because they have no papa. Since the genocide, lots of girls have caught children on the fly, because there are many men moving from place to place who no longer have living wives, and they know about our money troubles.

The truth is that our minds are quite disturbed by the loss of our parents and families. We have no one to obey, no one to look after, no one to confide in or consult for advice. We never get scolded or encouraged anymore. We find ourselves without anyone with whom to imagine a future, without a shoulder where we can rest a heavy head on evenings of sadness. It is a terrible burden to live as a forlorn woman, a great distress. And loneliness may turn into suspicion. In Africa, even if you no longer have a house, or any family, or even if you can't raise a hoe anymore, you must at least feed the children. Or else you quickly lose your worth in the eyes of others.

At night I think of my family with regret. We had beautiful cows, we never lacked for clothes, there were many of us to farm and eat as a family and we felt the comfort of to-getherness. Today there is too much emptiness, too much pain to survive properly. In the evening, I sit with survivors who live nearby and we talk about the genocide. We fill in what happened, since each one lived it in different places. Myself, I feel wary of relating my bad life in Congo, that's why I make little arrangements with the truth, as you know. Still, the more I hear my companions speak of the slaughters in the district, the more worried I am. Hutus accuse Tutsis of being too arrogant and too tall, but these are only the words of hidden envy. On Kanazi, the Tutsis were not richer, more proud, or better schooled than the Hutus; their plots of land were the same size. It's just that the Tutsis were closer from family to family. But that is traditional, we prefer our own company. The importance Hutus give to ethnic groups is only a pretext for jealousy and greed.

When I go over to Kanazi, I see *interahamwe* from Congo back on their land. I know that a small crowd of killers will be getting out of prison. Many of them will never confess, they will want to try all over again one day as soon as they have regained their strength. I heard too much boasting and vengeful talk in the camps. I know that the minds of the Hutu farmers are dominated by the *interahamwe*, who promise them our lands, and mark our faces for death.

Time passes without hardly wanting to change a thing. I don't know why God lets a curse linger on the heads of the Tutsis, but whenever I think about that, the ideas won't fit together in my mind.

THE NICHES IN THE MEMORIALS

In Nyamata and N'tarama, the churches are the only buildings surrounded by iron railings topped with spikes. As if the two memorials on their premises required better protection than any other home or public building.

The project for the Nyamata Memorial was conceived when the first rainy season began. The remains of the people slaughtered around the church, hastily buried with bulldozers by the killers, were starting to heave up from the earth and be swept away by rushing rainwater. Feral dogs and cats were already fighting over these sites.

At the time, in the pillaged town, neither the authorities nor the leading citizens could finance any costly identification of the victims. Foreign donors, for their part, were concerned above all with the fate of the fugitives in the refugee camps abroad. That is why the inhabitants of Nyamata undertook to disinter the bodies with hoes and protect the bones by placing them in the church. As the months went by, to these corpses were added any remains, scattered and unidentifiable, discovered in fields, ditches, wells, pens, woods, and rivers. Thus was born the idea of the Memorial "to try," as

Innocent puts it, "despite our poverty, to give the forgotten victims at least some humble dignity."

A simple sign planted in front of the gate announces the Memorial. At the threshold of the church, the pungent odor of death waits in ambush. The concrete nave of the church is empty, feebly illuminated by sunlight filtering through holes in the roof. To the left, in plain sight on a table in a vaulted sacristy, like a macabre and emblematic sculpture, lie the entwined and mummified bodies of a mother and her child, still pierced by the wooden spikes used to mutilate them to death.

The Memorial was built behind the nave in a kind of burial vault at the bottom of some concrete steps, where the stench of death is suffocating. Sitting on the last step, visitors peer in the wan light at the remains laid out on shelves. Lined up at the top are some shrouded bodies that were found intact; the next shelf down holds skulls; lower still lie the sternums, pelvises, femurs. . . . These heaps of skulls are fascinating, of course. Their orbits all seem to be staring at you from the beyond. Many skulls show signs of fractures; some are even still transfixed by knives.

In all, sixty-four niches, on four levels, contain the bones of around twenty-five thousand victims. Beneath the church, a neon-lit crypt with tiled walls is almost finished. A few bodies are already on view there, in a less crude and more aseptic atmosphere, to accommodate particularly emotional visitors.

Twelve or thirteen miles away, in the church at N'tarama, the militias never bothered to dig mass graves because the church, built some distance from their homes, was off their beaten path. The thousands of bodies were abandoned out in the open during the genocide. Afterward it was too late for the survivors to come retrieve the remains of their relatives and friends, because the rains and animals had been hard at work. At first, therefore, people protected the site with iron fencing. Then they decided to keep it as it was, in remembrance. In other words, to leave all those corpses in situ, as they were at the moment of death, like a scene from Pompeii: piled up between the benches, beneath the altar, crumpled along the walls, in their dresses, pagnes, shorts, among the suitcases, eyeglasses, flipflops, shoes, aprons, jugs, basins, sheets, necklaces, books, foam mattresses, all steeped in the high reek of death. Later, because of the prohibitive cost of preservative materials, a shelter was built to store some of the skulls and bones scattered outside the church.

Today caretakers are posted at the doors of the two deconsecrated churches to welcome the countless V.I.P.s, foreign or Rwandan, and the teams of journalists who must now make pilgrimages there. These caretakers present for inspection bulky "visitors' books" filled with signatures and many phrases such as, "So we never forget!," "Our hearts are with you!," and as one might expect, multiple inscriptions of "Never again!," already familiar in another context.

In N'tarama, one of the guides is Marc Nsabimana. He is a retired soldier, and a Hutu. Shortly before the war, he had returned to farm some land in the area. Married to a Tutsi, he tried to save her and some of his friends. Among the Hutu villagers, he was a helpless witness to the slaughter in the church and the marshes. Since then he has abandoned farming to devote himself to the memory of the victims. Indifferent to the heat, he lives bundled up in an anorak and punctuates every sentence by nodding his head and repeating tirelessly, "How was it possible, how was it possible?" Addressing his audience, you think at first; talking to himself, you soon realize. The other guide is Thérèse, who lives a little farther down the hill and who is herself a church survivor. She is more talkative and, when not on duty, she may often be found at Marie's *cabaret*, The Widows' Corner, chatting with her girlfriends over a Primus, especially about her day's visitors: their nervousness, their dressy outfits, and the generosity or skimpiness of their tips.

As a sign of the times, or perhaps by coincidence, ever since the evacuation of the white priests that triggered the massacres in the churches, *muzungus* have almost disappeared from the region. In Kinyarwanda, the word *muzungu* means "a white person," especially in the mouths of curious kids, cheerful and amused whenever they hail one going by. But linguistically, *muzungu* means "one who takes the place of." With rare exceptions, the priests and the specialists and logistics experts of international organizations in Nyamata are Rwandans or Africans.

In Nyamata, the faithful have reopened the doors of a decrepit church abandoned ages ago. Along with her boarders Florence the confectioner, Gorette the cook, and Gaspard the captain of the Bugesera Soccer Club, that is where Édith Uwanyiligira now goes for Vespers and Sunday morning Mass to join all the friends with whom she prays and sings hymns.

Édith is a mother as cheerful as she is pious. Her gaiety and good nature can no longer be dampened (in public, at least) by any of life's tribulations. She is deeply devoted to the education of her two children. Her living room is permanently occupied by the faithful; her bedrooms, by scholarly boarders; her yard, by gabby or sanctimonious neighbor ladies; her terrace, by relatives; and her garden, by noisy local kids. Just before the massacres began, Édith left her home with her husband, Jean-de-Dieu, to flee across the devastated country, carrying her son Bertrand in her arms, and in her belly, a child who became her mischievous little Sandra.

ÉDITH UWANYILIGIRA,
34 Years Old, Teacher and School Bursar
Nyamata Gatare

Before, Papa was the deputy clerk in the sub-district of Kibwa, near Ruhengeri. He was well-paid, highly respected, and then one night he was unloaded with his family into the bush of Nyamata. Tutsis were constantly being trucked in from Byumba, from Gikongoro, from everywhere. They banded together to protect themselves from the lions and elephants, and sheltered in huts of cardboard. That's how I was born on N'tarama Hill.

I never felt completely safe as a little girl. Whenever the *inkotanyi* from Burundi would attack Rwanda, the soldiers had to kill Tutsis, as punishment, and since the Bugesera is next door to Burundi, they would kill more of us over here. Those killed would soon be replaced by Hutu farmers. But with them, we lived only a short distance away without any trouble. I have always had dear Hutu friends in our area.

The civil war got a grip on our hills in 1991. That year, my first baby did not manage to pass, and he died in my womb because the road to the hospital was too risky. That was the beginning of some very dangerous political years, which some men exploited to their heart's content.

Three years later, finally, when the president's plane went down, the radios told us to stay inside. At the time, we did not know what to think about our situation, but the Hutus in our area were also unsure about that, and like us, they waited. Then we heard the mayors, police, local officials, all fanning out into the bush to stir up the villagers by shouting orders like these: "What are you waiting for to exterminate these Tutsis as in Kigali? They're cockroaches!" And "There's no more room for the Tutsis, you must kill them any way you can!" Or "They're vipers—now is the moment to get rid of them! No one will be punished!" At the same time, the *interahamwe* and the soldiers from the barracks at Gako were busy killing the first culls of people, in a few houses marked with paint. And so, five days later, our Hutu friends turned their way of thinking against their Tutsi neighbors.

I was then reaching the end of a pregnancy and had taken shelter with a Hutu neighbor, a longtime friend. One morning he told me, "Édith, you are a sin that can become mortal: I don't want to die because of you. Go out into the bush, right now." So on April 14, my husband and I went down to the Akanyaru River and paid the ferryman handsomely to take us across. We set out on foot, going west on the road to Gitarama.

The killings had not yet begun in the center of town there, because the people of Gitarama hadn't really heard about the organized massacres. The Hutus were still confused, and their political parties were arguing among themselves. They didn't know who was supposed to start anything. We were living outdoors, huddled near the marketplace, eating a thin white paste of sorghum and living wretchedly. That's where I gave birth to my daughter Sandra, lying on the ground surrounded by people, without a roof to protect her from the sun, without even a tree to shield me from men's eyes.

One day, the Hutus told us, "Well, that's it: the killers are coming to get you." We took refuge in the Electrogas factory. Some young men showed up and shouted to the factory guards, "We've come to take delivery of the Tutsis hiding on your property!" The guards pointed their weapons at them. But after the men went away, the chief guard was sweating uncontrollably. He loaded us into a small van and let us out in a ditch. We set off for Kabgayi: my husband, my son, my newborn, two sisters, a servant girl, and me.

During our flight, we kept silent, as if in humiliation. Wherever we went, we heard, "There are some Tutsis! Why are they walking upright when they should be lying dead?" Or, "Look at those Tutsis—how bad they smell. We have to kill them, we must get rid of them." Even the smallest schoolchildren we saw along the way would throw stones at us and shout, "They're Tutsis, they're cockroaches!" And they'd run over to their parents to warn them: "A group of Tutsis just went by, from the Bugesera! We know where they're going. . . ."

We ourselves were not ashamed of our dirtiness or our poverty; the only thing we felt was the humiliation of fear. We never thought about being filthy, about having no money, but we were terrified of losing our lives. And so we shivered, hearing those cries, because anyone shouting them could kill us just like that, in front of everybody, right by the road. Even if we felt guilty for not feeding our children, our first fear was of dying. Because a boy barely twelve years old could stab us with a knife, if he felt like it, without a word of reproach from his parents.

We found Kabgayi swarming with refugees, and again we slept out in the open. Tutsis fleeing the genocide in their districts mingled with Hutus running from the advances of the RPF at the border. So, one day, it had to happen: Hutu refugees began to kill Tutsi refugees, to the applause of the *interahamwe*. In Kabgayi, there were Hutu government ministers, Tutsi civil servants, Hutu and Tutsi bishops, and foreign photographers who had come to take pictures in complete safety of how Tutsis were being killed in the streets.

It was a miserable task to find any scraps to eat. We were hungry and crawling with lice. But, here is a lesson from nature: famished and germ-ridden, the children refused to get sick—because of the risk of slaughter!

And then, in early June, Satan himself arrived in the city. Here is what he ordered. Each day, soldiers had to park a bus near the refugee sites and fill it with Tutsis. Priests, nuns, teachers, shopkeepers—they began with important people. They would take about fifty passengers off into the bush and in the evening, the bus would come back empty. On June 29, they took away my husband. His name was Jean-de-Dieu Nkurunziza, "John-of-God." He was a brilliant intellectual and a most affectionate, considerate man.

Ever since that day, each night when I go to bed, I think of him. I think of my mother next, and my father, my brothers and sisters, my parents-in-law, and all who were killed. Then my thoughts return to my dead husband, until sleep is willing to come to me.

My husband and I always felt as happy as newlyweds together. We had loved each other since childhood. We grew up within five hundred yards of one another, on the same hill. After high school, we fell in love for real and got married. The day of my wedding, I showed off in a white dress edged with lace, just like in photographs. There was a whole crowd of elegant and joyful guests. My husband and I had more than enough love; I was capricious, and he loved me too much—he didn't even want me to do any housework. After high school, I continued my studies in Kigali, then returned to my husband's house in N'tarama, where he was a teacher, and I taught at the grammar school in Cyugaro. Truly, I was very well set with my husband, my parents, and my parents-in-law, who all spoiled me so much.

The genocide left me both a widow and an orphan. I was twenty-seven. One thing that torments me beyond sadness is that I don't know how my husband died, and I did not bury him. That's what eats at me day and night. Because they made him get on that bus, and no one can tell me how he was killed. If I had seen him dead, if I had any information about his final journey or his last words to his family, if I had given him a Christian burial, then, perhaps, I would be able to accept his disappearance more calmly.

Four days after his death, the soldiers of the RPF reached Kabgayi. I made my way back to N'tarama in sorrow. The neighbors were dead, my two older brothers had gone, the house had been burned, and the bush had reclaimed the fields, so I decided to go live in Nyamata. Now I don't want to spend even one morning in N'tarama, I'm so afraid of meeting my memories.

In Nyamata as well there were dead bodies strewn everywhere when I arrived: in the church, the streets, the thickets, in every home. If you went into the fields looking for food, or followed a path into the woods, you stumbled over corpses. We breathed deeply of death. People were desperately unhappy, trapped in sad agony because they could not stop thinking about those whom they had watched die. Many folks suffered from stinking wounds; there was nothing left to eat, nothing to bargain for or with—there were really too many problems and not enough solutions.

Ever since our return, I had been facing a barren future, too. I had a child and a baby, orphans pouring into my yard from all sides, I was on my own, falling sick, without any way to get to the clinic anymore, unable to find a way to cope with everything. Overwhelmed by the bitterness of my life, I wanted to just let go.

Then, I don't know how, I began to pray. I began quite timidly, and I went to church, where I chanted in a singsong, then sang my head off. I understood that God was calling me because from that moment on, He would be my support. That's it: I realized that I had been too selfish and naive before, that God had wanted me to draw close to Him. I now know that thanks to Him, I shall want for nothing, and I no longer complain because my husband was killed. God? I had not thought about Him before, because I was too spoiled, but now He will love and help me. This is my experience.

In the Bible, we read that the Jews of Egypt suffered greatly from the harshness and the forced labors of Pharaoh. They also endured many deaths, because of mistreatment by the Egyptians. God heard their murmuring, He listened to them, He prepared them for their return to the pleasant land of Canaan. As for the Tutsis of Rwanda, they received nothing as good as that along their path. I see no comparison between the Jews, who were the people of God, and the Tutsis, who are no one's chosen people. But because we saw many among us killed, because we still remained alive when everyone wanted us to die, that helps us to encounter God.

I would like to point out another incentive: during the genocide, the survivors lost their confidence and trust along with everything else, and that confuses them more than they realize. They may doubt anything: strangers, colleagues, even their surviving neighbors. On their own, they will struggle too hard to regain enough of that confidence to return among their fellows, but fortunately God helps them in this.

In my opinion, there is nothing special about the Tutsis. In our house, when Hutus came visiting, no word ever set us apart. Once we were all the same, except of course that the Tutsis raised livestock. A few Hutus also bought cows, but they called themselves Tutsis. It was during the last colonial period that the Whites ruined the hearts of the Hutus. According to what my grandparents told me, harmful lessons were taught in school from the early grades on. Whites were telling Hutus, "Look at those Tutsis: they have a king, they have favorites, they have cows. They think themselves superior. They are arrogant and want you to become their servants." So, the Hutus planned to strike back. Ever since Independence, there have always been Hutu propagandists to foment distrust and revenge. The colonizers had never counseled genocide, because that word was never taught. But evil lessons were doubtless cooked up by Rwandan intellectuals.

Today, when I listen to the radio, I hear that the Whites take off in warplanes as soon as there's a squabble in Iraq or Yugoslavia. In Rwanda, the bloodletting went on for three months, and the Whites sent only journalists on foot to get some good pictures. Whites mistrust Tutsis and Jews alike. With their arms crossed, they watched them die almost to the last one, and that's the truth. There's the real comparison between the genocides, and this problem will erupt again tomorrow because their suspicions lie buried at the bottom of their thoughts.

In Nyamata, it's remarkable how people no longer visit one another as before. Many poor souls have withered after surviving the ordeals of the war. They say, "The Hutus tried many times to kill me, and now nothing else can ever happen to me." They think, "I'm a widow, I'm an orphan, I have no more home, no more work, no transportation, my health is gone, I'm alone facing too many problems and I don't ever want to look at the world around me again." People withdraw inside themselves, dragging their personal pain off into a corner as if they were each the sole survivor, without caring that this pain is the same for everyone. The men spend more hours than ever at the *cabaret*, but without any exchange of ideas. The women can wait at home for a month without a visit from other families. A man can let three months pass without going to see how a younger sister is doing, and if the news isn't good, he just comes on home. Family bonds have been broken, as if everyone wished to keep their remaining rations of life to themselves from now on.

In my memory, the genocide was yesterday, or rather, last year, and it will always be just last year, because I can detect no change that will allow time to return to its proper place. The children are choosing the wrong direction as well: even school kids who never saw the murders, they listen behind walls to conversations, they hear all sorts of curses, and then you see them answering back to grown-ups, "You, if you bother me, I'll hit you with a machete," and they won't listen to anything in class.

Understand this: the genocide will not fade from our minds. Time will hold on to the memories, it will never spare more than a tiny place for the solace of the soul. Me, I've found refuge in the Church, since I found hope nowhere else. In church, I meet Hutus and Tutsis who pray all mixed in together. I continue to frequent some good Hutu friends. I know that all the Hutus who killed so calmly cannot be sincere when they beg pardon, even of the Lord. For them, the Tutsi will always be their enemy.

But I myself am ready to forgive. It is not a denial of the harm they did, not a betrayal of the Tutsis, not an easy way out. It is so that I will not suffer my whole life long asking myself why they tried to cut me. I do not want to live in remorse and fear from being Tutsi. If I do not forgive them, it is I alone who suffers and frets and cannot sleep. I yearn for peace in my body. I really must find tranquility. I have to sweep fear far away from me, even if I do not believe the soothing words of others.

I personally feel no need to talk constantly about the genocide, like the rest of the survivors. When my boy Bertrand asks me, "Where's Papa?," I tell him that he was killed. "Who did it?" "The *interahamwe*," I say, and I explain who they are, and that they killed his uncles and grandparents in the marshes and the fields, that they are men and women of great cruelty who will never go on a rampage again. When he sees uniformed prisoners outside the jail, he asks, "Are those the ones who killed Papa?" I tell him no, that his papa was killed far from here by other *interahamwe*, that he must not consider these men as criminals. To reassure him I add, "We were supposed to die because no one wanted us to live. We ought to have died, because I was a woman with a child and a newborn who couldn't run. But we did not die, thanks to God." If he talks to me about punishment, I tell him that a genocide goes beyond human laws. I say that no ordinary justice is lucid enough to pass judgment after such a thing, which only divine justice can do. I try to satisfy him with that. I don't want the genocide inscribed on my heart for all to see.

I also worry about the other people around me: exiles who have returned from Burundi to breathe life back into the Bugesera, Hutus who had no hand in the killings, little children born after the bloodshed. We must not ruin their lives by feeding them our nightmares. I don't like listening to all those memories of killings that get passed around again and again by small groups in the evening or on weekends. I no longer want to learn any more about the marshes. I don't appreciate it when people come to my house to talk over those times, in ever more tragic detail.

I don't want to marry a survivor so that I can take up the usual life of a woman who escaped the genocide. I prefer prayers and hymns. I would rather learn to play the guitar. I prefer to commune with Heaven, among friends. I think about my husband every day, in silence; I believe that no man will offer me the happiness he brought me. I also believe that, if he had not died, I would not have met God.

I only agreed to speak with you today about the genocide because you came a long way to reach Nyamata, because I have understood your need to hear what we lived through during that time, and your desire to learn how I'm supposed to survive such sorrows.

A Clarification Along the Way

At this point in the book, the reader might wonder at reading only the stories of survivors. In Nyamata, moreover, the mayor, the chief prosecutor, some teachers back from exile, former prisoners from Rilima, Hutu farmers—guilty or innocent, bystanders or heroes—and some survivors themselves did suggest that I seek out other kinds of witnesses. The reason for my refusal is simple.

Early in the 1990s, after the first military successes of a Tutsi rebellion based in Uganda, a majority of the political class, the army, and the Hutu intelligentsia in Rwanda conceived a plan to exterminate the Tutsi population and certain important Hutu democrats. Beginning on April 7, 1994, for four to fourteen weeks, depending on the region, an astoundingly massive segment of the Hutu population grabbed machetes—whether they wanted to or not—and started killing. All foreigners, including humanitarian officials and civilian and military professional aid workers, had been sent to safety. Rare indeed, and appalled by the events, were the journalists who ventured out into the country, only to be largely ignored on their return.

After May, this genocide was followed by several telegenic episodes: a Dantean exodus of about two million Hutus, shepherded by the *interahamwe* militias, all fleeing reprisals, and the simultaneous conquest of the country by the rebel troops of the RPF, who had invaded from the Ugandan bush. Then in November 1996, two and a half years later, came the sudden and unexpected return of Hutu refugees, provoked by the strategic, vengeful, and quite murderous raids of the Tutsi RPF troops on the refugee camps, raids that even penetrated deep into the Congolese forests of Kivu.

There were very few foreign journalists in Rwanda during the Tutsi genocide in the spring of 1994, but a horde of them arrived to follow the Hutu refugee columns to the Congolese border that summer. This imbalance of information; the ambiguous motives behind the refugees' flight; the dramatic aspects of those long, exhausting marches; and the hard line taken by the new leaders in Kigali all created confusion in the attitude of the West, which practically forgot about the survivors of the genocide clinging miserably to life out in the bush, and focused exclusively on the Hutu "victims" escaping along the roads to the camps in Congo.

On a trip to Rwanda during this exodus, I was struck by how withdrawn the survivors seemed in the accounts I was hearing. On a second trip three years later, in Nyamata, their mutism astonished me even more. The silence and isolation of the survivors, on their hills, were baffling. As I noted in my introduction, I recalled that only after a long time, when countless works by others on the Holocaust had already appeared, had the survivors of the Nazi concentration camps been willing and able to be heard and read, and I remembered how essential the survivors' stories had been for any attempt to understand that genocide. During the first discussions with Sylvie Umubyeyi, and then Jeannette Ayinkamiye and others brought forward by Sylvie, I understood immediately the importance of listening to survivors.

My stay in Nyamata took place over several months, interrupted by periods of reflection in Paris, where I worked on the interviews and my notes and prepared new questions for my informants. A room in Édith's house awaited me in Nyamata, along with an all-terrain vehicle rented from one of the beer merchants, Monsieur Chicago, and a tape recorder. Awakening at dawn to the shouts of a band of kids, morning appointment with Innocent or Sylvie, expedition into the bush to visit someone. Noon break, and another foray out to the homesteads. Late afternoons free—for playing with the kids or transcribing the tapes, word for word, for the interesting conversations and the pleasant music of the voices. The evenings: beers in a *cabaret*, chez Sylvie, or Marie-Louise, or Francine in Kibungo, or Marie in Kanzenze, to chat with friends. Weekends: more exclusively devoted to writing, listening to choir groups, and watching soccer matches. Unexpected encounters, a friendly visit from the photographer Raymond Depardon, or festivities sometimes altered this Spartan schedule.

I simply went looking for the stories of survivors, in the heart of this rolling countryside of marshes and banana groves.

Some memories comprise hesitations or errors, pointed out by the survivors themselves, but these do not affect the truth of their narratives, so essential to any understanding of this genocide. That is why there are no statements from political or judicial notables in Nyamata or Kigali, or testimony from former *interahamwe* leaders or killers interviewed in the Rilima Penitentiary or abroad.[14] For the same reason, I have not presented the viewpoints of any Hutu rebels or foreign protagonists in this drama.

After that clarification, we now return to a path through a eucalyptus forest near N'tarama, accompanied by the trilling of the *inyombya*, that faithful forest companion with the forked tail of trailing blue feathers. We walk up a steep path that plunges into a half-wild banana grove; an exuberant bunch of kids erupts from behind a hedge. In a courtyard, a young woman in a field pagne is resting, leaning back against the wall of the house, her legs outstretched, a baby asleep on her lap. Her name is Berthe Mwanankabandi.

She offers water from a large jug. Like others, she is quite surprised to find that foreigners can be interested in her story and the genocide; she explains, like others, that she no longer believes in the value of bearing witness, but she expresses no wariness, quite the contrary. She agrees immediately to talk, all morning long, in a soft voice.

Like many of the women who live nearby, she never complains, never raises her voice, shows no bitterness or hatred, conceals any distrust she might feel for a white man, and restrains, through silences, any feelings of sadness or grief. When the time comes that afternoon to go work in the fields, she offers to continue her narrative later on. The following week—and one, two, six months later—she is still as concise as ever because, she explains, she is thus compelled to clarify some of her thoughts, out loud, for herself.

BERTHE MWANANKABANDI,
20 Years Old, Farmer
Rugarama Hill (Kanzenze)

I was born into a crowd of nine sisters and two brothers. When little, we went through the forest in a parade of children to the school in Cyugaro. There was never any room on the benches for ethnic grumbling. Even when there were troubling massacres in the neighboring area of Rulindo, we were forbidden to talk about it among ourselves. Even when we could hear youths training for battle near the bridge over the Akanyaru, we could not show a worried face. We wrapped our fears in leaves of silence.

The day the plane crashed, we huddled in our houses, listening to bands of *interahamwe* out hunting from hill to hill, making an uproar. In a banana grove below our house, I heard the news that our elderly neighbor named Candali had just been killed. We immediately went down in a family procession to the church in N'tarama, since Christians, supposedly, respected places of worship. Three days we waited for feelings to calm down. We believed we really would return to our homesteads, but this time, the *interahamwe* arrived.

They sent youths into the little park all around the church, then began throwing grenades to blow holes in the walls. They came in singing—at first we thought they had gone crazy. They brandished machetes or axes and spears, and they were shouting, "Here we are, here we are, and this is how to prepare Tutsi meat!"

Behind the church, the boldest among us slipped away through the surrounding trees. Running blindly, we finally reached the marshes of Nyamwiza. That evening rain just poured down, and we took shelter in the school at Cyugaro, in the eucalyptus forest near the marshes. That would become our routine for a month: the marshes, the school, the marshes. Later, in that school, I learned how Mama and Papa had sighed their last breath. Until the end they pined for their native hill near Byumba, where they'd been robbed of their home before coming here to plant beans.

Each morning, I prepared food for the children with things dug from the fields. Then I led them down early, so they could conceal themselves under the papyrus leaves along with any adults who had exhausted their strength. On sunny days, we had to change our hiding places, because of footprints left in the dried mud. When the slaughterers arrived, they would be singing, and it was our turn to spread out through the swamp. They came at around nine o'clock, sometimes ten or eleven, if they didn't want to work too much. Some days, they were disguised as devils, wearing headdresses of leaves and pagnes tied as capes around their shoulders. Sometimes, stepping quietly, they tried to surprise us, but we'd hear the cries of macaque monkeys fleeing at their approach.

When they caught a family, they'd strike the papa first, the mama next, the children last, so that everyone could watch everything properly. They used to leave promptly at around four-thirty, because they wanted to get home before dark.

Then the lucky fugitives would come out and check the hiding places, trying to find those who'd been killed. The strongest climbed up to the school, to seek shelter and enjoy a bit of communal life. The weakest just lay down to dry off beneath the closest trees. As for us, our house was nearby, so we used to roam our fields at night collecting food. We tried to share any news about the neighbors we'd seen that day.

In the marshes, the acquaintance with whom you had hidden for many long days could disappear one evening without your knowing if the person had simply fled in another direction, behind another team, or had been plain cut down. We didn't know a thing about many of the missing. Didn't know whether we would meet them again soon, or whether they'd already come to a bad end.

I can say that we gradually got used to suddenly losing track of people, because we were focused elsewhere, on not getting caught—here and now—with our teams. Sometimes we didn't even notice the disappearance of someone with whom we'd shared school benches or *urwagwa* for years and years. For a few people, despair ruined even feelings of friendship and intimacy. Sunk in misery and fear, it became hard for them not to always think only of themselves.

After the food chores were finished, we'd huddle together or look after the ailing. Lack of sleep and food gave us a bad time in the marshes; dysentery and all sorts of diarrheas wrung us out. But malaria, on the contrary, usually so tenacious, was kinder to us, and I'm still amazed by that. Not only malaria: around us few companions were complaining about their usual ills, head- or bellyaches, or cramps for the women. Out of solidarity, amid all our misfortunes, those discomforts seemed to offer us a little period of grace.

On the evening of April 30, I discovered the bloody remains of Roseline and Catherine, my two little sisters. That night, I gave in to overwhelming grief. Later on, I sometimes lost control in the marshes when I'd see that they'd killed some small children, or some dear neighbors, or when we'd hear the moans of those who had been hacked into pieces.

I caught myself asking to die. And yet, I never stood up from my hiding place when I sensed that hunters were nearby. When they were passing, I could no longer command my muscles, which refused to budge. At the last moment, they could not agree to move so that someone would come slit my throat. Just as other people, whom we saw through the foliage, could not hold back one last gesture, raising their arms above their heads to ward off the machete blow that would kill them outright, even though the ensuing rain of cuts would make them suffer much longer. In our heart of hearts, there crouches a tiny desire for survival that will not listen to anyone.

When the *inkotanyi* liberated us, one afternoon, they escorted us in a herd of filth to Nyamata. I have no other words for it. I was dressed like a raggedy thing, in scraps of cloth shredded by branches. We advanced in a slow-motion dream, because we were walking in broad daylight, but not forced to run now for fear of being cut.

That evening, in Nyamata, some young people caught a goat. They lighted a fire, and handed me a brochette. Then, I tasted roast meat; I relaxed; I ate very slowly. . . . I stretched out calmly on a mattress, closed my eyes, and finally felt I was myself again.

I lasted three months in the camp. My head was almost empty, I couldn't feel my intelligence anymore. Mostly, I dozed. Our liberators were saying that the threat of massacres had vanished forever from our lives, that we had won. But whispering among ourselves, we said we didn't know what we could possibly have won, since we had lost the heart of life. Then I decided to go back to Rugarama to live at home, even though my parents would never return. Joining some neighbors, I ventured out into the hills, looking for sheet metal and doors abandoned beneath the trees by fleeing Hutus. The bush was eating up farmland everywhere, the fields had to be cleared all over again—it was most discouraging, but the children were pushing us forward.

Counting those in Claudine's house next door, eight little children went back along the path to school in N'tarama, and the four oldest of us now till the fields, except for whoever's taking care of the infants. Me, I caught a baby from a man on the fly. The child's name is Tuyishime, which means "Son."

At six every morning, we grown-ups leave for the fields, and return around eleven to heat some food. We freshen up and take a short nap, then go back to finish our work, coming home at five or so to fetch water. Myself, if the genocide hadn't stopped me, I would be a nurse. I deeply regret not having that job and its advantages.

At home, memories of the genocide crop up constantly in our conversations, but my sudden flashbacks to the marshes are growing rare—the faces of the unlucky dead, the mud, the dangers of that genocide time. More and more often I revisit life from before, with my family, when people were alive, around the house and on paths through the hills. I remember how I was so contented among my relatives and neighbors. But recalling those good moments from the past doesn't ease my sorrow. On the contrary, I believe that those who remember only the genocide, who think and speak of nothing but that, are steeped in misfortune, but at least less tormented by regret and anxiety.

Now, I see that life has become too backbreaking on the hills, where the land has grown too hard for hope to spring up. The genocide pushes into isolation those it could not push into death. Some people have lost the taste for kindness. The woman who has given birth and seen her children killed, the man who has built his house and watched it burn, the man who pastured his cows of lovely colors and knows they have been boiled in cooking pots—how can you imagine them getting up empty-handed each morning from now on? There are even people who have gone bitter through and through. For example, if your cow wanders into some man's field to eat, he screams at you that he'll refuse to come to an agreement over the damage because he has lost his whole family, menacing you over a trifle.

Still, the little children sadden me the most. They've seen all those dead bodies everywhere, they're scared of anything and nothing, and they don't care spit about the rest. One day I even heard some children playing *interahamwe*, and they were threatening to kill one another. These are dreadful shadows returning to their minds in disguise.

Before, we did not exchange gifts with the Hutus where we lived, but we shared the local brew and we talked together properly—and then one day they called us snakes. That became a most serious accusation, which may have pushed them over the edge.

During the massacre in the church at N'tarama, I recognized two Hutu neighbors who murdered like champions. They died in Congo. In the marshes I also recognized a farmer from nearby, who used a spear during the slaughter. He left in the march to Congo and returned in the same procession two years later. He waited at home for the soldiers and told them he no longer remembered what he had done. He was sentenced to death. I don't know whether they will shoot him one day on a hill; in any case, I won't bother to go see. Really, nothing like that comforts me enough.

Here is what I think. Those who just wanted to steal our homesteads, they could simply have chased us off, the way they'd managed to do with our parents and grandparents in the North. Why cut us as well? There are Hutus who slit the throats of their Tutsi wives and their only half-Tutsi children. Many never tried to hide these crimes. On the contrary, some even killed on their own thresholds before a small audience to show that they were trustworthy Hutus, and to win praise from the *interahamwe*.

Before, I knew that man could kill men since he killed them all the time. Now I know that even the person with whom you dipped your hands into a plate of food, or with whom you slept, he can kill you with no trouble. An evil person can kill you with his teeth, that is what I have learned since the genocide, and my eyes no longer gaze the same on the face of the world.

When I hear news on the radio of all those African wars, I fear the end is coming for Africa. African leaders settle their affairs too brutally. It is an insurmountable problem for us little people. But the case of Rwanda goes beyond African customs. An African massacres from anger or hunger in the belly. Or he slaughters just enough to seize diamonds or the like. He does not massacre with a full stomach and a peaceful heart on hills covered with bean fields, like the *interahamwe*, who I believe mislearned a lesson from elsewhere, outside of Africa. I do not know who planted the idea of the genocide. No, I am not saying it was the colonists. Truly, I do not know who, but it was not an African.

And I do not understand why the Whites watched us for so long, while we were put to the machete day after day. You who saw the genocide on television screens—if you don't know why the Whites didn't make the slightest protest, how could I, who hid in the marshes, ever hope to explain that?

I don't understand why some suffering faces, like those of the Hutus in Congo or the fugitives in Kosovo, inspire pity in foreigners while Tutsi faces, even sliced by machetes, provoke nothing but careless indifference. I am not sure that I comprehend or believe in the compassion of a foreigner. Maybe the Tutsis were simply hidden too far from the road, or perhaps they don't have the right sort of faces to express such feelings.

In any case, what the Hutus did is diabolical, the kind of thing that doesn't bear talking about. That is why, as long as there are *interahamwe* and their followers locked up in Rilima, I will always tremble whenever I hear voices raised among the leaves of the banana groves.

CLAUDINE'S *TERRE-TÔLE* HOUSE

The steep clay path up to Claudine Kayitesi's house plunges into the jumble of a banana grove and emerges before a flowering hedge. Her little house is of "non-durable" construction. In the Bugesera, dwellings are classified as non-durable, semi-durable, and durable depending on the construction of their walls—in other words, respectively, built from dried mud plastered on an armature of tree trunks, sun-dried bricks of mud mixed with straw and covered with pebble-dash or cement, or fired brick or cinder blocks. The roofs are usually mismatched sheets of corrugated metal, anchored by stones, or new metal roofing screwed down in overlapping sheets. There are some deep fissures in the walls of Claudine's house, which her father built at least ten years ago, but unlike the neighboring house of her friend Berthe, Claudine's doesn't flood in the heavy downpours of the rainy season.

The first room is whitewashed, furnished with a low table and two chairs, and decorated with several bouquets of freshly picked flowers. This is where the family waits out any rainstorms. A panel of cloth divides the main area from a back room containing two plank beds. On a table sit a Bible, a communion crown of artificial flowers displayed in a basket, a charcoal-heated iron, and a sewing kit. This is the room of Claudine and Eugénie, her younger sister, who is helping her raise the children. On the right, a small, windowless storeroom holds sacks of beans, bags of salt and rice, a jug, and a bar of soap. There's no sign of any candy or cookies. A travel bag full of clothes serves as a closet. The storeroom opens onto another bedroom with a mattress set on a platform shaped from the earthen floor itself. Here sleep the children: Jean-Petit, Joséphine, and thin little Nadine, a few months old.

No picture, no calendar or old poster decorates the walls as in Berthe's or Jeannette's house. Like the courtyard, the dirt floor is meticulously clean, thanks to a broom of leaves.

Outside, a superb settee of rustic woodwork and a bench are set along the wall. That's where everyone chats when it's not raining. The yard, round and spacious, is protected by a euphorbia hedge on which laundry and cloths are laid out to dry. In the shade of avocado trees, a square of greenery framed by flowerbeds and overhung by fragrant yellow bushes welcomes the evening gatherings. At the far end of the yard, a lattice-work of branches serves as shelves for a collection of pots, cups, and thermoses donated by humanitarian associations, as well as the buckets everyone uses while bathing to rinse one another off. The kitchen is in a *terre-tôle* hut too small to stand up in. Beans and bananas, the staples of both meals today, are cooking in an enormous pan over a wood fire. Tomorrow it will be beans and manioc, and the day after that, beans and corn. To Rwandans, a day without beans is no day at all.

The pen for the cow and calf, next to the kitchen, is constructed from thick branches stuck into the ground. The cow is scrawny, because after they get back from school, the children don't have time to take her out to graze her fill. She produces little milk. Without at least four or five cows, it isn't profitable to hire a young herd boy. Claudine explains that she can't risk slipping her cow into a cattleman's herd because in case of an escapade in someone's field, she could not pay for the damage. The calf is no more chubby than its mother, but he's lively. Two or three hens peck peevishly at one another on the dung heap; their chicks have a hard time surviving the feral cats. Behind the kitchen, at the edge of the banana grove, is the *terre-tôle* outhouse.

The closest houses belong to Berthe and, three hundred yards farther down the path, to Gilbert and Rodrigue, two teenage brothers who survived together in the marshes. The spring is a little over six hundred yards from Claudine's house.

At sunset, the family gathers around a kerosene lamp concocted from a metal flask and a twist of cotton. From dawn to dusk, the house is cheered by an extraordinary concert of birdsong, by turns playful and languorous. Still, Claudine dreams of a radio or even a cassette player to help pass the long evening hours. She also dreams of a bicycle that would allow her to carry her shopping and water cans up from N'tarama, take her stems of bananas down to the market, and above all go more often to Nyamata, to visit people and have some fun.

Neither the drought that sears her banana plants, nor the cares of her large family, nor the difficulties of her "man's work" ever draw the slightest complaint from Claudine or dampen her winning personality.

CLAUDINE KAYITESI,
21 Years Old, Farmer
Rugarama Hill (*Kanzenze*)

It's a fact that here, the genocide lasted from eleven in the morning on April 11 to two in the afternoon on May 14. I was in my eighth and last year at the school in Nyirarukobwa when it reached us. It taught me two lessons. The first is that there is no word in Kinyarwanda for the crimes committed by genocidal killers, a word whose meaning would surpass "wickedness," "ferocity," and similar feelings we can name. I don't know if you have such a word in the French vocabulary.

I find the second lesson a bitter one, although it's not the end of the world. It's that there are survivors, sometimes those who have suffered overmuch, who later on can quarrel with one another—like those others—for greedy reasons. Even if they have shared raw manioc and a miserable plight, searched for lice and vermin on one another's heads and backs, and been like the children of one big family, poverty and ingratitude can separate them. As if that more than vital bond in the marshes had dried up any future possibility of mutual aid and kindness.

Before that fateful April, our farmers had been worried about grim hearsay of the war. When we went to draw water, we'd hear neighboring Hutus lacing their chatter with remarks like "The Tutsis are beginning to crawl like snakes; soon they'll finish under our heels," and other intimidations. Merry bands would chant threats along the paths. In their hands I'd see gleaming machetes not for dirtying in the banana groves, so I was expecting a quick worsening of affairs.

When I heard that the plane had crashed, I joined other fugitives in the forest of Kinkwi. We tried to defend ourselves throwing stones, but we were overmatched and fled our properties to take refuge with everyone in the church. When the first grenade exploded, I was near the back door, thank goodness, and managed to sneak away. Knowing the hills were in the hands of the *interahamwe*, I ran toward the marshes, this way and that, never looking back. I could hear other fugitives in the thickets. The marshes we knew by reputation—we'd never gone near them before because of the mosquitoes and snakes and the boundless mistrust they inspired. That day, without slowing down for a second, we dove on our bellies into the mire.

At night, the eucalyptus forest seemed quiet, so we walked to Cyugaro. The luckiest of the fugitives in the banana groves gradually managed to join us. Our schedule for survival was established. At dawn, we went down into the swamp and made our way through the papyrus. To avoid all dying together, we divided into small teams. We'd place three children here, two children farther along, two more somewhere else. We increased our chances, took our positions lying in the mud, surrounding ourselves with foliage. Before the attackers arrived, we shared ideas for dodging fear; afterward, we couldn't even whisper anymore. We drank the muddy marsh water. It was enriched, pardon my bluntness, with the blood of the dead.

It wasn't hard to hear the *interahamwe* from a long way off. They whistled and sang, shooting their guns into the air, but oh, they were careful not to waste bullets killing people outright. In the beginning, they would crouch down and murmur gently to lure us out: "Little one," or "Mama, come on out, we see you. . . ." Well, even those so scared they couldn't help obeying, they weren't rewarded with a quick gunshot. Reason why, later on, neither the sick, nor the infants, nor anyone ever moved at all until the whistle blew for the killers' departure.

In the evening, as Berthe told you, we fixed food for the children, and we ate as much as we could find: manioc, yams, bananas, to regain strength and hold out through the next day. Since we couldn't carry anything with us into the marshes in our hands, we carried our provisions in our bellies, so to speak. We put the children to bed in the animal pens or the kitchen shed, never in the house. We spoke quietly to avoid attracting the killers' attention. We would describe the bodies we had seen during the day, and how they had been cut; we'd determine who hadn't emerged from the marsh, and thus discover who had been caught that day. And we'd wonder who would be killed tomorrow. After the first killing sessions, we no longer asked ourselves why we had to die. That question had become irrelevant. But we thought a

lot about the how of it. We tried to imagine what the suffering was like, dying under the machete. In any case, I was
personally quite worried about that.

We never found any reason to quarrel, since all we thought
of was death, and the need to help one another. We took turns
sleeping. At around five in the morning, we'd start back down
the path, quite calmly, because we knew the *interahamwe* were
asleep. On the edge of the marsh, we would wait for sunrise
and the attacks we knew were coming. We wore the same torn
clothes and no longer felt ashamed because we knew we were
all alike. We helped one another pick pounds of lice out of
our hair. The mosquitoes bit us eagerly at times, but in a way,
our muddy filthiness somewhat shielded us from malaria. We
lasted in that wild existence. We were forgotten by time,
which must have continued to pass for others—Hutus, foreigners, animals—but no longer wished to pass for us. Time
didn't bother with us because it no longer believed in us, and
we, therefore, now hoped for nothing from time. So we were
waiting for . . . nothing.

Some days, when the killers caught a small group, they
would take a girl away, without killing her immediately, to
rape her at home. That's how some girls lasted a few nights
longer, thanks to their beauty. It's against custom for our men
to be the killer of a girl they've forced, because they fear
bringing down a curse by mixing the two emotions. Afterward, however, other colleagues would cut the girls and heave
their bodies into ditches.

On certain days, when the Hutus worked mostly on the
other side of the marsh, we could talk and even eat a little

extra survival ration. The next day, they would work our side intensely, so that we hardly dared breathe and the children risked being consumed by hunger.

The criminals didn't bury their victims, because the enormous numbers discouraged them. They preferred to finish the task of killing, without the added fatigue of cleaning up the mess. Those people were too sure of getting rid of all the Tutsis. They figured that no one would ever again come looking into their affairs in Rwanda.

On April 30, in fact, they came down from every direction to attack on all sides. That throng was quite excited by their ambitious intention to kill straight through the noonday break. That evening, thousands of people lay dead and dying all through the swamp. I was so discouraged, I thought about letting myself just lie down in the waters of the marsh, but I still didn't dare simply wait for the machete. I don't know anyone who killed himself. I think we were too busy trying to save ourselves to waste time with such thoughts. I've never met anyone who claims to be ashamed of surviving—just a few people who feel troubled about matters like not doing something vital, one day, when they easily could have.

To hear the Whites tell it, the genocide is supposedly a fit of madness, but that's not true. It's a project that is meticulously planned and properly carried out. If you listen to some Hutu neighbors, they claim they killed a few people when threatened with death themselves. That's true only of a small number. Because a lazy farmer's field will not grow green by itself, and a careless driver's truck will break down, but in the marshes, you could count dozens of corpses without noticing any idleness or negligence on the part of our Hutu countrymen.

The truth is that many Hutus could not bear the Tutsis anymore. Why? That stubborn question haunts the banana groves. Me, I can see there are differences between the two groups that make the Hutus resentful. Tutsis sometimes have longer necks and straighter noses. Their faces are thinner, in a way. They are more sober of disposition and affected in their manner. A Hutu wouldn't think twice about going straight from his field to see someone in an office or clinic, while a Tutsi would change clothes. But as to wealth and intelligence, there is no difference at all. Many Hutus distrust a so-called malice in the Tutsi character that simply does not exist.

Hutus also say that we had too many cows. That wasn't true. My parents kept no cattle. Our neighbors raised no cattle, and their families were larger and more needy. Cows at the market are there to be bought by anyone with the money to buy them. The truth is that Hutus don't like the company of cattle. When a Tutsi spots a herd of cows in a grove of trees, he sees good fortune. A Hutu, when he runs into some cows, he sees only trouble and trampling hoofs.

Hutus also used to mutter, "Tutsis are arrogant, they don't want to marry Hutus, they don't want to offer dowries to Hutu families." But a Tutsi girl who follows a husband to a Hutu hill, she won't feel safe if the Hutus begin killing the local Tutsis, and she will return to her family alone and empty-handed.

The way I see it, the Hutu extremists simply cut the Tutsis to shorten our women, who are too tall for their taste, and to eat our herds, which require all that grass, and to snatch our land. Reasons why Hutus accuse Tutsis unjustly of being swarming cockroaches.

I often think that we are the forgotten people of Africa. We live in French Africa, but the French approve only of the Hutus. I don't know why Whites mistrust the Tutsis. Perhaps because Tutsis take charge of their own education and they're less open, more reserved. Myself, I see that Whites are scandalized by the genocide, but privately they say that the Tutsis brought it on themselves a little, through their behavior toward the Hutus or some idea like that. Whites do not want to see what they cannot believe, and they could not believe a genocide because that is a slaughter that overwhelms everyone, including them.

Still, we must remember a much more important truth: our African brothers did not lift one finger more than the Whites to save our lives, and yet, given our customs and linguistic heritage, who better than Blacks to understand the misfortunes of their fellows? Because of that cold-heartedness, we will remain alone on the hills, feeling vaguely oppressed.

But I congratulate myself anyway on being Tutsi, because otherwise I'd be a Hutu.

Just once, I returned to the marshes with a friend, to see again those muddy hiding places where she and I lived, the slimy pools where all those other companions died. Then I simply never went back. Often, at night, images crowd in on me in dreams; I see faces that never speak, faces just staring at me, and when I awaken, I can feel some uneasiness between me and those who were cut. No, I do not feel guilty. I am not at fault, because there was nothing I could do for them. Still, I don't feel glad that I was lucky. I don't know how to explain this feeling, since it concerns a most intimate relationship between me and people who are no longer alive. I'm upset and quite distressed when I think of them. I'm not simply sad, as with the ordinary dead.

I work at farming to feed the children. We're ten children without parents, in our two houses, and I'm the eldest. A neighbor found us a cow that has already given us a calf and also provides a bit of milk for the little ones, plus manure for the banana grove. On Saturdays, I work as a mason's helper in N'tarama to earn a few coins, and I receive some aid from the Survivors' Fund.

When I walk by the church with the Memorial, I don't like to look at all those nameless bones. Sometimes, though, I do show foreigners and other visitors who are lost how to get there, and then I can't help staring at the skulls. They're disturbing, those empty eye-sockets of people who are perhaps not at rest, after what they suffered, and who cannot bury their humiliation beneath the earth.

Often, when the *interahamwe* had killed someone, they would take any clothes in good condition. And in a way, when we found those bodies all naked and cut into pieces, bodies of oldsters, young girls, everyone's bodies, the sight of that nakedness burned our nerves brutally. Those nude bodies abandoned to time—they were no longer completely themselves, and we were not yet them. They were a waking nightmare. . . . I don't think that you can understand.

Sometimes I go pray in a church, because I was fortunate enough to be baptized. From now on I ask only one thing of God: to help me keep from becoming mean to those who inflicted such evil on us. That's all, really. I don't want to taste revenge.

I won't say that I will definitely never marry. But what man would want to give his money to feed all these unclaimed children who eat in my house? In Africa, when you are sunk in misfortune, a friend comes to bring you a drink; he comforts you with gentle words, takes endless trouble to cheer you up, tends to your health if you're feverish, but as to giving money, that's quite different. In Africa, family blood is so important regarding the division of material things. Outside the family, it's easier to hand out kind words than paper money.

I often see myself back in the old days, with Mama and Papa, my brothers and sisters; I think of the school benches, the books I caressed with the palm of my hand, the teaching career I hoped for, and then it's so hard to keep life from losing all savor. Before, I loved to read stories in books. Today, time hardly ever helps me out: I no longer have the chance to read, never find the slightest little book. I don't think the genocide changed my personality, except that I must often be alone, and that can trouble me. When I find myself too isolated, with sad thoughts all around, I get up and go find my neighbors, children on their own like us, and we listen to theater pieces on the radio, which I really like. They make us imagine characters far away and all their harmless adventures.

I think that in spite of everything, it's good to talk about what happened. Even if it's deeply painful, for us survivors, to stir up those memories in front of foreigners, and even if the truth cannot reach into the hardest hearts. But I cannot offer you any particularly helpful ideas about the cause of the genocide.

I think, moreover, that no one will ever line up the truths of this mysterious tragedy and write them down—not the professors in Kigali and Europe, not the groups of intellectuals and politicians. Every explanation will give way on one side or another, like a wobbly table. A genocide is a poisonous bush that grows not from two or three roots, but from a whole tangle that has moldered underground without anyone noticing.

Myself, I waste no more thought trying to understand my former neighbors. I sometimes joke about all that to put on a good face, while my lips know they are lying to my heart. I am so torn apart by that curse, but I hold it inside, I keep it from overwhelming me, I stay calm for the children.

Twilight at La Permanence

In the evening, in Nyarumazi, soon after the sun has vanished into the marshes of Rulindo beyond the Akanyaru River, men leave their houses and meet in the former grain warehouse, where they sit on low stools or on the ground, leaning back against the walls. One of them sets a jerry can of *urwagwa* down in the middle of the room, sticks a straw into the opening, and the men take turns crouching by the can to suck up long swallows. In the darkness, they talk about the time before the war, when Nyarumazi—near a forest of heveas, halfway between N'tarama and Kibungo—was humming with business. They speak as well of the women who are no longer there, and of those who are no longer as they were. They tease the mechanic who has recently sold off his last jack, and make fun of the radio that has just died of failing batteries. Then they drink without talking anymore and later, they stagger on home or doze off, sagging against the warehouse wall.

Stars in a limpid sky are the only lights over the hamlet. Along the dirt track leading down from Nyarumazi to the main thoroughfare pass silent silhouettes in small groups, sometimes speaking very softly, as if to avoid disturbing the sleep of the banana groves. In the middle of the night, in the Bugesera, the narrowest path is never deserted. People are constantly climbing back up to their hills: civil servants returning late from a meeting, jackets slung over their shoulders; farmers who lingered at a *cabaret* over a last Primus; women slowed down by the children carried in cloth slings on their backs or by sacks of beans piled on their heads. The monotonous calling of cuckoos cuts through the lowing of cattle and the strident *tio ooo* of wakeful gonoleks.[15] Leaning on staves, many elderly villagers have been slowly walking along, the woman behind the man, since early that afternoon. Other folks are already leaving in the darkness to catch a ride at dawn on a truck bound for Kigali.

On the outskirts of Nyamata, in the Gatare neighborhood, the croaking of frogs from pond to pond creates a thundering cacophony. Glowing coals illuminate gatherings in yards; children roam though the bushes. On the soccer field, kids play around a single goal in the gloom, taking advantage for as long as possible of a real leather ball, on loan from the older boys until morning.

On the main street, just as the wind was dropping, the red dust settled when darkness fell. The last vehicles have been parked behind their fences; the goats tied up in the little market are dozing. On the square, teenagers are chatting or listening to music in front of the beauty parlors. Mopeds transport couples clinging tightly together from love or the jarring ride over the rough road. Pale neon lights gleam in the *cabarets*. Sitting on a crate beneath an awning at his warehouse, Monsieur Chicago watches cases of beer being loaded for delivery. Chicago is one of the few stout men in town, which has probably earned him his nickname and his good humor. With a staple remover, he uncaps bottles he slips into your hand like stolen goods. He survived the massacres by crossing the country on foot from Gikongoro, a city to the south, where he never returned to pick up his former life.

Parked across from the intersection is Théoneste's new van, the first one since the war. Théoneste is wearing a mustache and clothes in the "Kigali diaspora" style. He was the region's most respected tailor in the old days, when important men and their wives wore fashionable suits and chic boubous. He was one of the "Kayumba Forest Track Team," along with Innocent, Dominique (one of the directors of the rehab center), Benoît the debonair cowboy, and the rest of those twenty who outran the opposition. As for Théoneste, on his third attempt he accomplished the virtually unique feat of escaping from the hill all the way to the border with Burundi. That miraculous exploit is probably what fuels his constant and infectious bursts of laughter. His place is always full of drinkers. One arcade down, neon letters announce the entrance to Le Club, the rendezvous of youths from the well-to-do families of Burundi, who remember with nostalgia their nights in Bujumbura.

Still on the main street, a blue cloth banner stretched between two stakes announces the grand opening of a new restaurant, La Permanence. The walls are painted jade green; the embroidered tablecloths are cut from pagne fabric. The owner is Sylvie Umubyeyi. She's there only in the evenings, to chat a bit with the customers and keep an eye on the business, because during the day she's off in the bush.

Sylvie's most striking feature is the serene beauty of her sparkling black eyes. Her delightful voice is also seductive, like the elegance of her language, as when she replies, when asked how she thinks of such lovely phrases, "They just come to me, because if you've made it back from out there, then you have truly seen life laid bare."

Sylvie is a survivor from Butare, a university town in southwest Rwanda. When she arrived in Nyamata, at the end of the genocide, she knew no one here. The countryside was devastated, deserted, littered with the dead. Sylvie has been a social worker in these hills ever since, going out each morning with her team to invent a unique profession.

She sets out early in a van across fields, through thickets and banana groves, making her way through forests, searching for children who emerged alive from the marshes, or returned from the camps in Congo, and are now hiding behind mud walls, wandering through bean fields or the bush. She visits them, registers them, opens a dialogue with them, and sets out again.

When she approaches an adobe hut, she calls out politely to announce her presence, and shakes hands with all the children who pour out of the nearby groves and farm plots. She visits an animal pen, inspects a leaky roof, checks out school notebooks and uniforms, asks after the hen, talks planting, insomnia, checks on runaways with the little children and teenagers. She sits on a tree trunk, chatting in a relaxed and playful voice, listening, unconcerned by the passage of time. A leather-bound memo book and a Bic pen she fiddles with constantly are the tools of her trade. Beneath her cheerful manner, Sylvie is practical, demanding, and meticulous.

With her savings she bought a cow for each of her five children, and she has just opened that restaurant, La Permanence, to help support the extended family she now houses. She overflows with energy because she loves her work. She likes pretty clothes because she "isn't getting any younger," and each day she wears a different outfit: a flowered dress, tight jeans, or a brightly-colored pagne. She presents a merry face to the world, which she views with amazing lucidity. When she tells her story, she sometimes pinches the bridge of her nose and listens for a long moment to the chirping of the crickets, to hold back her tears.

SYLVIE UMUBYEYI,

34 Years Old, Social Worker
Nyamata Gatare

Three or four families had gathered together in a large vehicle to make the journey, and we took the road to Kirundo.
It was toward the end of June. I myself was a survivor of
Butare, but I had no hopes of getting as far as home, because
the killings there were still going on.

In those days, it was too early to think about heading to
any other district, so we crossed the Bugesera, which I'd
never seen before. It was the first region to enjoy a little
security, because the genocide had just been stopped there.
The Bugesera looked like a huge desert. You couldn't go out
into the surrounding areas yet, and passengers who went any
distance from the road, to forage for food in the fields, for
example, could not do so on their own for fear of marauding
interahamwe.

When we arrived in Nyamata, that was as far as we could
go, so we got off at the town hall. We searched for lodgings,
one or two families per room. Before the war, Nyamata was
said to be a nice little town, but the moment I saw it I knew

they'd had too much war, too many houses burned, too many people scarred and sickened. The town was beyond filthy. What it lacked most of all was people. On the road I'd learned about the massacres in the churches, and I knew that almost all the inhabitants had disappeared, as in Butare. My immediate impression was that our lot here would be a harsh one.

We also swiftly discovered in detail just how disrupted everyone's existence was, as if they were all struggling to find their way completely on their own. You could tell that no one gave a hoot about anything, that they no longer saw any future ahead, all hope had gone, and people's minds seemed crippled. Here's an example. We happened to enter a dilapidated home to pay a goodwill visit and found a small family lying on the ground. We asked the man, "You, why are you sleeping like that, in all this dust and mess, without taking care of your family?" Without even getting up, he answered, "I don't care anymore. I had a wife, she's dead. I had a house, it's smashed. I had children, some were killed. I've lost everything I loved."

As for me, I'd made the journey with my husband, my two children, some little brothers and sisters, and an infant born during the genocide. I spent the first three months in Nyamata almost without leaving the house, coping with daily chores. Life was so hard because there was nothing. You could spend four or five hours without finding even a full bucket of drinking water—same thing for food, or wood.

It wasn't a problem of not knowing anyone in the area, because we had arrived with a small group of people we knew in Butare, and no one here even seemed to recognize anyone, either. Later, in September, I learned that a Canadian organization was looking for a female social worker. I went for an interview, and landed the job. I began going out into the hills. And then I saw life laid bare.

At the time, few vehicles were still operating in town. One of them would drop us off at eight in the morning in the bush—where we would set out on foot—and return for us at the same place at five that afternoon. That's how we began to track down the unaccompanied children, meaning those without any relatives or adults with them, kids who'd been scattered throughout the hills by the slaughter. We're still at it today. We keep visiting homes, we enter the banana groves, we identify the children who've gathered together or who sometimes live alone in little shacks, without even a blanket or something to sit on.

Meeting those children touches me deeply, because no matter which way they turn, their plight is dreadful. They all escaped from different situations: some survived in sorghum fields, some in the marshes or at the bottom of a ditch, some traveled a great distance, outside the country, along roads thick with ambushes. These children are deeply shaken, but not all in the same way. There are those who want to talk but cannot organize their thoughts well enough; those who cannot express themselves, quite simply, through anything but tears; and those who say, "I cried already, but they killed my papa and mama anyway. I cried but I've got nothing to eat, no roof over my head. I cried but I haven't anything for going to school. Now I no longer even want to cry—not for me, not for anybody."

There are children who would talk with no trouble right after the genocide, but who have now fallen silent. They don't see the point of talking anymore. At first, they spoke of the slaughter as if telling terrible and extraordinary stories, tales that were of vast importance, but that would end with their own telling, or that would end well if their audience listened to them closely. Later, the children's hopes faded away with their words. Time has made them realize how their lives have changed, and how true these stories are. The children keep dwelling on what they lived through in the marshes, they understand that no one will ever replace those they've lost, and they shut themselves up inside a silent bad dream. Some are very frustrated, or confused, or rebellious. So, I gradually adjusted myself to them.

To throw a line out to someone who has been beaten down, you must first encourage that person to open up a little and dare to express a few thoughts, which will reveal the knots of inner anxiety. My strategy for that is simple. I approach that person, I observe a little moment of silence, I begin to talk, and I say, "I, too, am a survivor. I, too, was marked for death in every possible way. I, too, know that my parents are dead, and I saw *interahamwe* a few yards away from me sticking spears through people. I, too, lived through all that. And both of us will live from now on with these truths." That way, the person begins to feel more comfortable with me, and able to grow in trust and self-confidence.

Genocide is unlike any other torment. That is a certainty I've gathered from hill to hill. Sharing the genocide in words with someone who lived it is quite different from sharing it with someone who only learned about it elsewhere. In the aftermath of a genocide, there remains, buried in the survivor's mind, a wound that can never show itself in broad daylight, before the eyes of others. We survivors, we don't know the precise nature of the hidden wound, but at least we know it exists. Those who haven't experienced the genocide—they see nothing. If they make a real effort, they will one day accept the fact of this secret wound inside us. But that will take quite a while, even if those people are Rwandan or Burundian Tutsis, even if they lost families and close relatives in the killings. I cannot explain why, but I know this process will be slow indeed. I'm not familiar with the history of other genocides, but I suspect that this delay was present there as well: those who have not gone through genocide, even if they try sincerely, will take a long time to understand more than just a bit of it.

It is also vital, with a child coming out of genocide, to provide immediately for some desperate material needs. To find medicines if the child is sick, obtain a room in a house, give food, clothing, perhaps school supplies, and tools if the child will be farming. In this way, a child feels less abandoned, more respected, and more comfortable within society. The child must then be nudged toward other children. Children speak easily among themselves about their experiences, and that unlocks language. Then you must listen to everything everyone says, to help each child figure out his or her problem and find new words for even deeper insights.

I should clarify an important observation: the genocide has changed the meaning of certain words in the language of survivors, while other words have flatly lost their meaning, and anyone who listens must be wary of these changes.

In any case, I have noticed over time that the very youngest children are not the most vulnerable after a genocide because when they begin to taste life again, they recover themselves more spontaneously. Their pleasure is still lively. Except, of course, if they have been gravely traumatized and have stopped speaking.

The most difficult ages are adolescence and old age. The adolescents, they suffer more than others from not understanding. They cannot accept that the *interahamwe* tried to exterminate them without any previous provocation or quarrel. The teenagers were stepping jauntily up to the gates of life—only to be beaten back with machetes. Ever since, they have been mired in the *why* of this. They wonder, "Since I didn't do anything to the Hutus, what is it about me that they can't stand, what does my appearance show without my realizing it? Why did they have to massacre my parents who were just quietly farming? How am I going to live near people who think only of killing me without any explanation?" Adult life becomes too confusing for many teens—for all those girls, for example, who nowadays wind up pregnant any old way, casually, obliviously, without any thought or care for the baby's tomorrows.

Still, when adolescents get together, when they speak about this among themselves, they do listen to one another, sharing their feelings, and that helps ease their anxieties. A few even start talking to young Hutus, and such conversations provide some faint hope.

As for their elders, they are inconsolable over their losses. They had raised children who gave them food, clothing, sweet comfort in their old age, and now they are left without a soul around them. Killing their children was like hacking their arms and legs off at the threshold of the last stage of their lives. The old folks keep saying, "I'd brought up healthy sons and daughters, I'd married them off properly, and they died in the marshes. Who will take my arm now to guide me through old age? Who will help me escape sickness and sorrow?" These people now see only loneliness and poverty ahead for company. It's really so hard for them not to drown their thoughts in the abyss of memory.

There are also Hutu children who walked all the way to Congo and have come back home. The difference here is virtually invisible—except that the children of this long journey can never stay still: they tend to drop out of school or leave their families abruptly and head for the street, and they love to disappear into the woods. When you speak with them, when you ask them how they left for Congo, with whom they traveled, what their time in the camps forced upon them, how they're living now, they'll tell you several things, blurt out a few details, but they'll run into some word or other and whoops!— you've lost them: they don't want to continue the conversation.

The children who survived in the Nyamwiza Marsh have gazed into the black heart of evil, but for a limited time. If you can get a grip on them, and pull gently, they will come to you more easily.

The ones who went to Congo lived in confusion and danger for a very long time. In the camps in Goma, they were on their own for everything: not a soul took care of them anymore, they felt rejected by everyone, and returned like the lowest of the low. They are no longer at home in their own skins.

Those who survived the genocide will never get rid of what they went through, but they can make their way back to real life because they can tell the truth, and they are surrounded by people who tell the truth. They fear many dangers, but they are not threatened by lies.

The children who come back from Congo, well, they live inside silence, and they don't look people in the eye when they talk to them. Some have parents who died or vanished during their flight. These children say they know nothing. Some of them have parents in prison; when you ask them if they know why, they wriggle out of the questions, replying that they were sick, they weren't there, they didn't see or hear anything while the genocide was going on. They are perpetually terrified that a word will slip out—and then someone will come for them, too. And even if they dare say something, even if they want some relief from their burden, if they try to reveal what they know, they don't tell the truth. They concoct alibis to prove that they never saw a thing. They're afraid of being mistreated. And I'm not mistaken when I say that as the years go by, they feel more and more guilty for their parents' evil deeds.

The problems of Tutsi children who survived the slaughter evolve over time. Their memories, too heavy to bear, grow lighter nevertheless, because they change as the children grow up.

For Hutu youngsters who went to Congo, the oppression remains, because they are not facing the past. This silence is paralyzing them with fright. Time is rejecting them. From visit to visit, I find no change. One can see that anxiety is forever stifling their thoughts. It is such hard work, encouraging them to speak, but they can never set foot back in life if they do not talk about what they must confront within themselves. So you must be very patient and gentle with them, and visit them regularly, entrusting time with the birth of friendship. In a few families I have been visiting since the beginning, the children have recounted what happened during the genocide, what they saw with their own eyes around the house in those days, and the harm their parents did. Now they seem more at ease with the children of survivors, whom they are starting to get to know.

Often, children stumble into a hole of grief or panic, especially during sleep. They reproduce in dreams what they lived through; they cry out, weep, sometimes they begin to run through the shadows or beg to be forgiven. That disturbs the other children in the house and everyone spends a sleepless night waiting for morning. When little ones or adolescents lose control in a crisis, someone must sit by their side and ask if they want to talk about it. If I'm there, I begin talking; so do they. I tell about everything that happened to me, they recount their own experiences, as I already explained to you, and meanwhile the child calms down. I pass over some parts of my ordeal, but I remain ready for questions. Too bad if I can't explain why it happened—the main thing is always that the child should feel less alone for having survived.

Myself, I like talking about it all with the children, with friends and colleagues. In any case, not a day goes by that I don't remember those things, so it's useful to discuss them. A genocide is a film projected every day before the eyes of the survivors, and there's no point in interrupting it before the end. I love my work, it doesn't exhaust me; on the contrary. I go all out on the job. Talking with the children helps me deepen my understanding of the genocide.

My tiniest children, I treat them differently, because the moment for talking hasn't arrived yet. If I were to tell them about the dangers I escaped, my words might infect them with a sorrow, a hatred, a frustration that little children cannot handle. I would risk the irruption of feelings that would be alienating. It's important to accept this, because if children have not lived through the killings, they should not suffer the same damage as their parents. Even if life has come to a halt for someone, it continues for that person's children. When my children are more grown-up, I will answer the questions they'll bring home from school. I won't hide anything from them, because the genocide is written in the history of Rwanda. But I want life to stretch out in front of them for a long time before that blood appears.

I was born in the prefecture of Butare. My father was a librarian at the National University of Rwanda, and my mother was a grammar school teacher. There were nine of us children; I was the second oldest. Our extended family included more than two hundred people living in a dozen houses lined up on a street in Runyinya, a neighborhood lying eleven miles from the city center. I grew up in a lovely family. I was surrounded by grandparents and the relatives you call aunts and uncles. I never heard my parents have a single argument. They earned a little money, and we didn't have to buy much because we had our own bit of farmland. My life was carefree, so I was quite happy. I completed my humanities courses and began studying the social sciences, intending to go to college. I married an up-and-coming teacher, lived in an average house, tended my little flower garden. Really, life was good.

In Butare, Tutsis and Hutus lived side by side without a hitch, especially in the neighborhoods favored by teachers. There was a small *cabaret* near our house where we had always talked together and shared brochettes of roast meat in friendship. This changed at the very last minute, at the news of the president's death. The day Habyarimana died, suddenly the colleagues with whom we'd shared gossip and a beer the day before no longer wanted to meet our eyes. On that day I realized how oblivious we'd been to the contempt those friends had felt for us.

In Tutsi families, we'd avoided any mention of the war between the soldiers from Uganda and Habyarimana's army. Maybe the Hutus talked about it a lot among themselves, feeding a hatred for us they had carefully kept secret. Really, I was so surprised I couldn't understand it at all.

So, after the plane crash, we were ordered to remain in our homes, unable even to go to market. We were guarded by soldiers and had no idea what would happen next, but we weren't being killed yet. On around April 9 or 10, the situation in the country deteriorated. We heard, on the radio or through rumors, that things were falling apart in Kigali, and there was dreadful news of bodies lying all along the roads in other regions. It was still calm where we were, however, although many people were beginning to starve in their homes. Meanwhile, we discussed the crisis, wondering about perplexing questions, such as: Since no one knew whether the plane crash was an accident or not, why did the Hutu peasants immediately march out in organized columns to kill Tutsi farmers?

One morning, the soldiers opened our doors to let us spend one day getting food. That was April 19. So my husband went to the market. When he returned, he told me, "It's truly serious in town—the *interahamwe* have started killing. We have to leave now." I was quite sick, weakened by my pregnancy, but I didn't protest. I told him, "Fine, I'll pack a suitcase." He said, "No, we haven't time anymore, we're getting out this minute." I put our diplomas into a small case with some things for the children and we left, in the clothes on our backs, our two children in our arms. We just happened to find seats in a van, splitting the cost with another family, and we went off toward Burundi, because Butare is close to the border.

And then, along the way, I discovered the ferocity of the war. I mean corpses just everywhere, people dying with their bodies split wide open, still writhing and moaning, and Hutus rejoicing in their viciousness. Near the customs office, we were held up at a last barrier. A vast throng of fugitives gradually piled up behind us, pouring out of the fields, emerging from the river, running down the road, all screaming. Soldiers and *interahamwe* were cutting them down absolutely nonstop. The criminals looked like savage hordes, really, leaving only the dead and dying in their wake.

So we sat down on the ground and waited for death. I had thrown off my fear. I was growing numb to the uproar of shrieking; I was waiting for the blade. Sometimes you are afraid when a situation arises, but as it develops you proceed under a kind of anesthesia. I had become patient. Suddenly, we heard a panicky little volley of gunfire. Some sort of dispute among the soldiers, I believe. I felt the baby in my womb, and thought of the mothers-to-be that had been sliced open with machetes; I grabbed one child by the hand, my husband hoisted the other one onto his back, and I ran without another thought through the mad carnage, straight into the arms of a Burundian customs official, who said something like this: "Well, madame, it's a happy ending for you, and now you must rest." A moment later, looking back, I saw bodies lying in a great sea stretching far behind the barrier.

I loved Butare very much. First because it was my birthplace, and then because I was used to it. It was an average city where I knew all sorts of people. Afterward, I returned to the house where my parents had been killed, to give them a Christian burial. I stayed there only long enough for that.

Before the war, a Rwandan couldn't live just anywhere, as in your country. He would insist, "I can't live in a place without my family, my house, my neighbors, my cows." If he went on a trip, he always returned to where his family had its roots. When I visit Butare now, it hurts me, because no life is left for me there. If you find no one you used to chat with where you once lived, you feel sad. No one lives in the outskirts of the city anymore. Downtown, I saw many new faces without spotting anyone I used to know. To their credit, many colleges, university departments, and graduate schools have reopened since the war, yet I still feel that intellectual life there has been shattered. I found only four people who'd been students with me; the others are dead. In our old neighborhood of Runyinya, the bush has moved into the ruins of our houses. Our big family had been about two hundred strong; now there aren't even twenty of us left.

In Butare, when I run into Hutus I used to know well, they avoid me, sidestepping me after our greeting and a few polite remarks, unwilling to begin a real conversation. Shame will immediately come between us, even if I don't show any bitterness, and even if that Hutu is a good person. I'll hear, "Excuse me, Sylvie, I'm really very busy," and things like that to cut our talk short.

In the customs of Rwanda, a neighbor is a most important person. Only your neighbor knows how you awakened, what you need, how to advise you, how we can help one another. If you no longer know your neighbors, or if they slip away when you talk to them, you feel a great loss, and you must leave. I cannot imagine any future for me in Butare now, because the things and people I once longed for there are gone.

After the genocide, it was therefore all the same to live anywhere, so you settled in where life had put you. As for me, I'm now capable of fitting into any society at all, if I find a job and a roof. In Nyamata, no one is where he or she belongs anymore. There are survivors from the area who can't return to their former lives, Tutsis back from exile in Burundi or Uganda, Hutu refugees from Congo who can't manage to feel at home. There is also great poverty, and poverty of mind as well. But as I often tell people who complain, anyone lucky enough to be alive somewhere after a genocide should dig in there and be grateful.

I personally feel that if anything good ever comes to me, it will be in Nyamata, because this is where I found myself again. In Nyamata, I roam the hills, talking with many people about their innermost feelings. I like these visits, these discussions. And I like to be with my children, fixing their meals, mending their clothing, that's all.

If I don't travel abroad, or buy the pretty dress I noticed in a shop window in Kigali, or get invited to a wedding, that doesn't bother me anymore the way it once did. I no longer covet what I don't have. I don't feel any desire or need to rush into things on the pretext that I almost died, that I might no longer have been here to do them. I still haven't even made myself a little flower garden like the one in Butare.

No, the war hasn't destroyed my peace of mind. I consider myself extraordinarily fortunate, because others moved heaven and earth to escape the machetes and yet they were killed, while I'm still alive. If I've been that lucky, then my enjoyment must carry me along at a calm pace that suits me, not too fast or slow. I watch time go by, without running after it—or letting it sneak away unnoticed.

Many people spend their days doing nothing, won't look for work anymore, won't build themselves a new home. They are overcome, crushed by mourning and the onslaught of misfortunes, no longer even looking for a way out.

Some people want life after the genocide to stand still so they won't need to question themselves anymore. They keep saying, "Why wasn't I able to save my mama? Why couldn't I save my child?" They're sick at heart for still being here, alive, alone. "The family was all together," they say, "and we heard the killers, we ran away, and when we came back, Mama and the children were lying cut up in their own blood." Many people feel guilty for being alive, or think they accidentally took a better person's place, or they simply feel worthless.

I, too, left many dear friends behind. I'm sometimes stricken with sorrow, but never with remorse. My parents died on April 8 and I didn't even know it at the time, because I couldn't open my door. On the day we fled, I saw many people dying behind us. And I'm alive, with nothing to reproach myself for.

It happened, it shouldn't have, but it happened. I grieve for my vanished friends. But even if they were chopped up with axes, even if they died gruesomely, that was their day to die, without me. What was I supposed to do? Panic? Stay and die with them? No. I tell myself, life is over for them, but not for me. I will simply think of them, of us, with sadness, my whole life long.

I have many dead around me, but I don't want to lose faith in life, because there are also the living. I don't like shelters where people give up and wail. It's the same weakness, whether one leaves Rwanda for fear of massacres or spends all day sitting and repeating, "If I make bricks for a house, they'll destroy it; if I sew some nice clothes, they'll tear them up," expecting nothing good, from oneself or others, huddling beneath a black cloud.

Of course I, too, often felt humiliated. I was part of an accomplished family that was almost completely destroyed. A fine future chose me, only to drop me flat. I'd intended to go to college but never did. I was a fugitive, a refugee, almost a beggar. I waited for someone to give me a pittance to eat, I lived in dirt and pity. But now I have set all that aside. If life goes on, it must go on absolutely! When my health isn't good, when my work seems too much for me, when disappointments await me all around the house, I don't care: every morning, I find my good humor where I can.

Deep inside me, nothing important has changed. My life has taken a new course, my neighbors are different now, my job isn't the one I studied for, but I want to be the same person. I'm not looking in the genocide for pretexts to give up or excuse myself. I don't know if you can understand me.

In Butare, I remember French soldiers who would jog by early in the morning, sweating in their new track suits. During the first days of the genocide, they took off, herding all the Whites in front of them. Why were they there, if they couldn't use their guns? Why did they take French leave, if they didn't know anything? I have no idea, but I do know that the Whites never wanted to face the genocide squarely.

As for the television cameramen and journalists, they came and traveled around. They took a look, but they saw only remarkable events, so to speak. They saw the columns of Hutus heading for Congo and observed, "Look, there are some victims of the war, fleeing certain death." They saw the army of the RPF entering the country and explained, "There are the Tutsi soldiers winning the ethnic war and driving out the Hutus." But the people who had hidden in the muck of the marshes, in the crawl spaces of houses, at the bottom of wells, unable to escape for weeks on end—there was no one to come worry about them. On television screens, reporters said, "Those who weren't killed are now trying not to die on their long journeys to the camps," and in the end they completely forgot about the survivors of the massacres.

So, these survivors, to whom could they speak? No one. They were caught between those coming in and those going out, and that shoved them even further aside. We found that barbaric. That callousness seemed cruel to us. We had survived the machetes for weeks, we had come through the worst without a single helping hand, and already we had ceased to matter at all. Even now, years later, that hasn't changed much. There are always hidden or poorly presented truths about the survivors that prevent foreigners from accepting the genocide without suspicion—in other words, from being alarmed by it.

I offer a little explanation: the Whites who calmly watched the genocide, they feel embarrassed by their lethargy, their deceit, so they now prefer to confuse the slaughters, to lump the wars and countries together, to avoid the simple truth and not have to deal with too many survivors. Then the survivors as well lose their respect for truth and think, Well, since those others arrange the truth to suit themselves, why pay any attention to them?

Another important observation is that it's difficult for a White to comprehend certain African attitudes. Here's a situation that can often arise here: I have a good neighbor, we seem fine, we're on good terms. One day, he becomes brusque with me, reproaching me for something but without saying what. He broods over this and his eyes turn cold. If I notice his evil eye in time, I go find a friend and tell him that something has come between the neighbor and myself. The friend visits the neighbor to talk to him. Perhaps he'll return to me and say, "Your neighbor, he's angry with you over this or that, be careful." Me, I'm either going to get right up and go give my neighbor an explanation, or I will keep out of his way. Otherwise a serious dispute might break out. If he bottles up anger, an African may suddenly explode in uncontrollable violence. This African character is what leads to unforeseen massacres. When they occur, Whites look at us and say, "Well, they're at it again: the Congolese—or Sierra-Leoneans, or Angolans—are killing one another, but it won't go on forever."

Still, in Rwanda, the Whites could not have failed to understand after a few days that this was no ordinary massacre, but a genocide, and they did nothing. That's why, in the future, they will leave a stain on the survivors to conceal their mistake.

When I discuss the cause of the genocide with friends, we come up with three ideas. The first has to do with poverty and the necessities of life. The second idea concerns ignorance. The third focuses on influential people—and all those who are easily influenced. Four out of five Rwandans cannot read, so it was no trouble to feed them evil thoughts that were to their material advantage. Before the war, I never noticed any appreciable difference between Tutsis and Hutus, since we socialized together, helped one another, shared a friendly glass. And one day, they brought out gleaming new machetes. They had certainly harbored a secret hatred they could no longer handle. But that explanation cannot justify extermination.

Ever since, I have been looking for some clue that I cannot find. I know Hutus did not feel at ease with Tutsis. They decided to erase them everywhere and forever, to feel more comfortable among themselves. But why? I have no answer. I do not know if I bear on my face or body some special marks they cannot stand. Sometimes I say no, that cannot be it—being tall and slender, with delicate, gentle features, all that silliness. Sometimes I say yes, that really is what began to grow deep inside them. It is an utter madness that even those who killed can no longer manage to contemplate. Still less those who were supposed to die.

On the hills, I sometimes speak with families who participated in the killings. They say that they regret what they did, what their men did. Their explanation? "We were told, 'Kill Tutsis, you'll have houses, you'll have farmland.' But no one knows how it could have happened." I don't understand them when they talk like that, but I can listen to them. I am deeply convinced that it isn't a question of forgiving or forgetting, but of reconciling. The White who let the killers work, there is nothing he can be forgiven for. The Hutu who massacred, there is nothing he can be forgiven for. Someone who watched a neighbor slit girls' bellies open to kill babies before their mamas' eyes, there is nothing he can be forgiven for. There is no point in wasting words talking to him about it. Only justice can pardon. First we must think about a justice for the survivors. A justice that makes room for truth, so that fear will drain away. A justice to reconcile us.

I have hope for the future, because things are on the move in the hills, people are timidly drawing closer to one another. One day, perhaps, the families of those who killed and those who were killed will live together again and help one another out as before. But for us, it is too late, because from now on there will always be a sense of loss. We had stepped forward into life, we were cut, and we retreated. It is too heartbreaking, for human beings, to find themselves fallen behind where they once were in life.

So far, I haven't met anyone who claims to be proud of having survived. No one who tells me, "Life is beautiful, and I never knew it was that beautiful until I was so scared of dying during the massacres"—like someone who has recovered from a dreadful illness, for example. Even if they have found a good life, have a job, lovely children, beer, survivors have been cut down in their very lives.

I do not know a single survivor who feels completely safe, forever free from terror. There are those who fear even the very hills where they should be working their lands. There are those afraid of meeting Hutus on the road. There are Hutus who saved Tutsis, but who no longer dare go home to their villages, for fear that no one will believe them. There are people scared of visitors, or the night. There are innocent people whose faces inspire fear and who dread inspiring fear, as if they had the faces of criminals. There is the fear of threats, the panic of memories.

I'll give you an example. Last week, we took the van into the bush to identify some children in a new sector. We lost track of the path in the foliage. I told the driver, "Well, we're lost, but we can press on anyway to finish things up." At the edge of a banana grove, we encountered a group of Hutu peasants at work. They stopped trimming branches, their arms motionless, and stared at us in silence. I heard myself shouting, "This is it, we're done for this time, we're all going to die!" I was beyond frightened—I no longer knew where I was, my vision had gone blurry, I thought we'd wandered into a nightmare. I was sobbing, repeating to the driver, "Don't you see them, all those men with their machetes?" Placing his hand on my arm, he said to me, "No, Sylvie, everything's okay. They're farmers pruning their grove." He did his best to calm me down. That was the first time since I've gone back into the bush that it caught up with me. I was in such anguish that day!

Often, I regret the time wasted thinking about this evil. I feel that fear is eating away at the time luck has saved for us. I tease myself by thinking, Fine, if someone still wants to cut me, let him go grab his machete. After all, I'm only a survivor: he'll be killing a person marked for death, and I amuse myself with that fantasy.

Because if you linger too long with the fear of genocide, you lose hope. You lose what you have managed to salvage from life. You risk contamination from a different madness.

When I think about the genocide, in a moment of calm, I mull over where to put it properly away in life, but I find no place. I simply mean that it is no longer anything human.

Written in Nyamata in April 2000

A FEW STATISTICS

The district of Nyamata comprises fifteen hills in an area of 154 square miles.

In March 1994, on the eve of the genocide, its population stood at about 119,000 inhabitants: approximately 60,000 Hutus and 59,000 Tutsis. The high proportion of Tutsis reflects the fact that the region, uninhabited during the first half of the century, was initially an area of refuge for massive influxes of Tutsis early in the 1960s.

Around 50,000 Tutsis—in other words, five out of six Tutsis—were murdered in the district of Nyamata between April 11 and May 14, 1994, when the RPF troops arrived. So it is plausible, as Innocent Rwililiza explains, that if the killers had not been delayed by looting and celebrations, they would have finished the job.

About 22,000 Tutsis, returning home chiefly from Burundi and Uganda, began settling in the region beginning in July 1994. Around 24,000 Hutus, on the other hand, have not returned from their exile in Congo.

Today the population stands at 67,000 inhabitants, plus around 6,000 local inmates in the penitentiary at Rilima.

The district has 13,386 registered orphans.

Several hundred thousand Tutsis were murdered in Rwanda in a period of fourteen weeks. Statistical research on a genocide is quite difficult because of the special nature of the evidence and personal testimony. It will therefore take a few years to confirm a more accurate estimate of the number of Rwandan genocide victims, just as it took several decades to confirm reasonably exact figures for the toll of Holocaust victims. For the moment, arguments over the precise numbers are of no interest.

NOTES*

Chronology of Events in Rwanda and the District of Nyamata

[1]*gaçaça* : Named after "the flattened grass under the elders' tree," these tribal courts render traditional justice. Faced with the collapse of its judiciary due to the death, flight, or complicity of so many judges during the genocide, the Rwandan government reactivated the *gaçaças* both to speed up the trials of persons suspected of participation in the genocide and to involve Rwandan citizens in the collective work of assigning and admitting individual responsibility for the massacres. At the level of the hills and towns, the *gaçaça* arraigns the accused in the community where the crime took place, and the local population gives testimony or passes judgment under the supervision of more or less professional officers. This judicial undertaking began in the spring of 2002, and the many assemblies have produced controversial results. Those suspected of the gravest crimes (ideologues, propagandists, high-ranking leaders, rapists, and well-known killers) may not be judged by *gaçaças*.

INTRODUCTION

[2]*cabaret* : The Rwandan *cabaret* may be an authentic tavern, with a proper sign and terrace, but is often a more humble combi-

239

nation of social club, bar, and general store. It might be simply a few thatched huts in someone's yard or a one-room shop with no sign, a floor of beaten earth, with cases of beer—especially Primus, a Belgian beer much prized in Rwanda—and soft drinks stacked against the back wall, and bottles and large cans of home-brewed banana and sorghum beer lined up behind the counter. The shop might stock a few groceries, some fabrics, household and hardware items, and so forth.

EARLY MORNING IN NYAMATA
Cassius Niyonsaba

[3]Memorial : Assuming that they would be the principal targets of Hutu violence, many Tutsi men fled to the hills when the 1994 genocide began. Women, children, and the elderly sought refuge in the churches that had always provided sanctuary in the past, but there they were horribly butchered, and two of those churches, at Nyamata and N'tarama, have been designated as genocide memorial sites.

[4]*interahamwe* ("Those who attack together") : These Hutu extremist militias, created by the Habyarimana clan in the early 1990s, were trained by the Rwandan army and sometimes received additional instruction from French soldiers. Their chief weapons were gleaming new machetes supplied in the thousands by government officials and the army. Tens of thousands of these activists recruited, trained, and led the citizen killers of the genocide.

THE BIG AND LITTLE MARKETS
Jeannette Ayinkamiye

[5]corrugated metal : In *Machete Season*, Hatzfeld devotes an entire chapter to corrugated metal, which the Belgians brought

to Rwanda after World War I to use as roofing for colonial buildings. With time, this material became the roofing of choice for even the most modest dwelling, the *terre-tôle*, or "sheet metal adobe." Used as a unit of measure (a house "of ten sheets") and of exchange (a nanny goat costs two sheets), sheet metal is the only element of a house villagers cannot make themselves, for rainy Rwanda does not provide thatching material. A dismantled roof is easily transported, and in 1994, sheet metal pillaged from Tutsi houses and then abandoned by exhausted Hutus fleeing into exile in Congo was sometimes collected by Tutsi survivors struggling to rebuild their homes.

THE BUGESERA ROAD
Francine Niyitegeka

[6]*awalé* : Also called *igisoro* in Rwanda (and familiar to American children as *mancala*), *awalé* belongs to a worldwide family of games played on a board with a series of holes usually arranged in two or four rows. The strategy of these "sowing games" is based on picking up all the seeds in a hole, then sowing them one at a time until one player has captured all the seeds in play.

[7]*inkotanyi* of the RPF : Known as "The Invincible," these Tutsi rebels were essentially exiled troops who organized in Uganda and other neighboring nations in 1988 to fight Habyarimana's dictatorship. They formed the basis of the Rwandan Patriotic Front, and began military operations against the Rwandan Army in 1990. On the opening day of the 1994 genocide, the RPF launched a vast offensive and by July 4 took definitive control of the country under the command of Paul Kagame, who later became president of the Republic of Rwanda. The RPF was subsequently reorganized into the regular Rwandan Army.

At the Widows' Corner
Angélique Mukamanzi

[8]sitatunga : This antelope of amphibian habits has an oily, water-repellent coat of chocolate or grayish brown, striped with white in the male. Its slender, splayed-out hoofs allow it to run swiftly through mire, but make its gait on dry land somewhat ungainly. The sitatunga feeds at dawn and dusk on papyrus leaves, and in case of danger can hide for hours, submerged in water with only its nose showing.

Bicycle-Taxis Under an Acacia
Innocent Rwililiza

[9]Boda-boda : Part of the African bicycle culture, the Boda-boda taxis began in the 1960s and '70s on the Kenyan-Ugandan border, where there was a no-man's-land between the border posts that people could cross without the paperwork required for motor vehicles. Bicycle owners would shout "Boda-boda" (border to border) to attract customers for their Indian or Chinese bicycles equipped with locally made cushions and carriers for customers and goods.

[10]Arusha Accords : The Arusha Peace Agreement was a set of five accords signed in August 1993 in Arusha, Tanzania, which—temporarily—ended the civil war between the Rwandan government and the RPF. The implementation of the power-sharing agreements of this cease-fire collapsed with the assassination of Habyarimana that unleashed the Rwandan genocide.

NOTES

A Secret Flight
Odette Mukamusoni

[11]**boyeste** : A girl domestic servant, the *boyeste* is the female equivalent of the traditional "boy."

[12]turquoise soldiers : The United Nations Assistance Mission in Rwanda was dispatched in November 1993 to supervise the implementation of the Arusha Peace Agreement, but its initial strength of 2,500 men under the command of the Canadian Major General Roméo Dallaire dropped to 450 men on April 14, 1994, a week after the killings had begun. UNAMIR's intervention consisted of protecting and evacuating expatriates and its own personnel. After French troops initiated and completed their own controversial Operation Turquoise in June and July, which was said to be a humanitarian mission but which principally protected the exodus of Hutus to Congo, a new UN mission, UNAMIR II, arrived in August, three months after the end of the genocide.

[13]**Christian name** : Every Rwandan baby is given a personal Rwandan name at birth, and when old enough to be baptized, receives a Western Christian first name.

A Clarification Along the Way
Berthe Mwanankabandi

[14]The testimony of these last is the subject of the author's book, *Machete Season: The Killers in Rwanda Speak.*

Twilight at La Permanence
Sylvie Umubyeyi

[15]**gonolek** : The gonolek, a bird with a remarkably sonorous call, is quite common on the hills of Rwanda. It has a scarlet belly, a jet-black cloak, and wears a jaunty yellow cap.

*Author's notes are distinguished from the translator's by a bold typeface.